Prized Possession

Prized Possession

"A Father's Journey in Raising his Daughter"

Alan Smyth
with Kristy Fox

authorHOUSE®

AuthorHouse™
1663 Liberty Drive
Bloomington, IN 47403
www.authorhouse.com
Phone: 1-800-839-8640

Published by AuthorHouse   04/30/2013

ISBN: 978-1-4817-4706-6 (sc)
ISBN: 978-1-4817-4705-9 (hc)
ISBN: 978-1-4817-4704-2 (e)

Library of Congress Control Number: 2013907594

Any people depicted in stock imagery provided by Thinkstock are models, and such images are being used for illustrative purposes only.
Certain stock imagery © Thinkstock.

This book is printed on acid-free paper.

Because of the dynamic nature of the Internet, any web addresses or links contained in this book may have changed since publication and may no longer be valid. The views expressed in this work are solely those of the author and do not necessarily reflect the views of the publisher, and the publisher hereby disclaims any responsibility for them.

Contents

Dedication

This book is dedicated to the scores of little girls out there who deserve better growing up. May this conversation make a difference for at least one of them.

And to my own "little girl" who allowed me to be her daddy even when I wasn't very good at it and trying to figure it all out. I couldn't be more proud of the woman you have become. Your heart, faith, humor and zeal for life are inspiring. You will always be my "Prized Possession."

A Pastor, A Father & A Writer

Rusty George—A Pastor

Lead Pastor, Real Life Church, Santa Clarita, CA

The content found on MyFatherDaughter.com as well as in the book "Prized Possession" is coming at just the right time. After reading this material, as a father with daughters, I have learned a lot about my role as dad as well as the pressures my daughters will face as they grow up. As pastor of Real Life Church, I am excited for my congregation to participate in this conversation because it is vitally important to families. There is both a huge void and a huge need within the church for this conversation. Alan Smyth and Kristy Fox bring unique experiences and expertise on the topic of being a dad of daughters as well as what adolescent girls need to thrive.

After attending the seminar "Prized Possession," which is based on the book of the same title, this was my text message to Alan Smyth:

"Perfect, Amazing, Awesome, You both did a phenomenal job!"

Jimmy Hagenbuch—A Father

I have spent a lot of time thinking and praying through my relationship with my daughters. I have felt inadequate in my leading of their lives and the ability to truly show them how much I cherish them. I feel like what you have given me has brought to life the longing to show Aubrey and Kaylee truly what they mean to me and Jesus. You have provided me with a spring board for excellence in the way that I raise, love and cherish them. The words on these pages gave me tangible things to act on and a vision for a greater relationship. Aubrey (7) and I have been having conversations about what it means to be 'Daddy's Prized Possession.' Every time we talk about it there is a glow about her and I know it touches something deep within her. This emphasizes the need she has for my voice in her life. Recently I spoke to Kaylee (5) about her being 'Daddy's Prized Possession.' As I was explaining to her who she is to me and the reasons why I love her and why she is my 'Prized Possession,' she literally had tears in her eyes. Kaylee is not normally able to pay close attention when I talk to her due to her hearing loss. However this time she was fully engaged and hung on to every word that I said.

The words that you and Kristy have put into my life have redirected the way that I will love the girls that have been entrusted to me as well as will help shape the view of women that my son will have as he watches me care for his sisters.

Donna Hatasaki—A Writer

Alan Smyth has a gift of telling the plain and simple truth in a clear and compelling way laced with good humor and wit. He's a "player/coach" leader in life, and he's a player/coach leader in this book. Dads who read it will feel like they've found a good friend who is in it with them, coaching them and encouraging them in the profoundly important arena of loving their daughters. If you're a dad and you want clear, practical advice along with substantial encouragement and support regarding your relationship with your daughter, read this book.

The content, tone and organization is awesome. Great, clear, compelling, funny, touching, simple, profound. Perfect.

"Prized Possession" from the Bible

"And we, out of all creation, became His prized possession"

James 1:18b, NLT

"Prized Possession" from the Dictionary:

"The biggest thing in your life, the one thing you couldn't imagine your life without"

"Something you care for deeply above all else"

"It could be anything you cherish close to your own heart and can be worth millions or worth nothing to someone else"

Real Talk

In between each chapter is a page entitled "Real Talk"

The anonymous quotes on these pages come directly from an array of women from various age groups. It is our attempt to further illustrate the gravity of this important conversation.

Falling Forward

"Everything *worth* having is expensive"
—*Oswald Chambers*

I have spent 20 plus years working with adolescents and their families in clinical and counseling settings. Most of the Fathers I have worked with during that time were decent men with good intentions. In truth, many of those dads got lost, distracted or discouraged somewhere in the process of trying to manage their schedules, responsibilities and relationships. They needed some practical advice, some healthy perspective and some wisdom that works in the real world. They needed what Alan offers us in *Prized Possession*.

Alan Smyth invites and challenges all fathers to make a deliberate choice in the ways they connect, protect and value their daughters. I have known Alan for 25 years and can assure you that he is the Real Deal. He has lived out, worked out and walked out the principles and practices shared in these pages. Alan shares much of his own journey in this book with both humility and conviction. He is not tossing out glib advice and casual reminders. He is calling us back to a core conviction and a foundational truth. The relationship between a Father and daughter is a central and unique feature in their development and well-being. What happens in this relationship will prove to be a blessing or a burden for most of their lives.

Alan has also gathered the voices and stories of other veteran dads' and their daughters. These are not Cookie Cutter accounts with sanitized or spiritualized relationships. These are men and families with hard earned, real life wisdom. *Prized Possession* offers highlights and insights from a wide range of fathers and daughters, both in triumph and tragedy. In all of these accounts, Alan captures and integrates the central themes and key components of healthy Father-Daughter relationships. Some men reading this book will be reminded of the Big Job and the Great Job they have as Dads with daughters. Others will get a sneak preview and a heads up for the road ahead. Both groups will be glad for the encouragement and insights offered in Alan's book.

Through my professional experience as well as my personal experience, I can assure you that this conversation is of paramount importance. Alan first brought me into the conversation surrounding this project via a long voice message. As I sat and listened to the message and heard his heart, I said out loud, "YES", "YES", "YES," to each point he was making. I later told Alan that this topic is at "ground zero" of importance for the healthy development of a daughter.

Nehemiah was an Old Testament leader living in hard times with big challenges. There were real enemies at the gate, there was damage to repair from a troubled past. The men doing the work were faithful but exhausted and there was still much to do. Nehemiah gathered the community leaders who were wobbling and wondering if it was all worth it. In Chapter 4, he reminds them why they are doing what they are doing. "Everything *worth* having is expensive," so what is worth having? Nehemiah calls out to them and to us with both an answer and a challenge, *"Remember the Lord who is great and awesome, and fight for your brothers, and your sons, and your daughters, your wives and your homes."*

Do you want a bargain? Go to Groupon or the Dollar store. If you want a resource, pick up Alan's book. If you want results, read it and do it. I promise you, your daughter is not a bargain, she is a treasure. Act accordingly.

Grace and Peace

Dr. Don Worcester Ed. D.

Chapter 1

25 Years in the Making

I didn't set out to write a book. I never intended to publish my thoughts regarding my father/daughter relationship. However, this book demands to be written, and I feel somehow compelled to organize and articulate my thoughts on this topic. So, reluctantly, I venture into the unknown world of authorship. With great humility, I step into the public arena. I hope and pray that the following words will be received by those in need and will ultimately make a difference in the lives of our girls.

This book didn't happen overnight. In fact, it was 25 years in the making. Why so long? Because my daughter, Brittany, is 25 years old today. It has been my absolute joy to be her dad all this time. A number of things have fallen into place to cause me to write this book. In fact, I have no other choice than to write it. I feel a great sense of responsibility with the topic of fathers and daughters and a drive to organize these important thoughts. It would be my joy to learn that, after reading this book, a light bulb went on in the heads of dads with daughters and of men who speak into the lives of young women. I'd love to hear that a parenting trajectory was changed because of this content. In fact, if this book positively impacts just one little girl, it will be worth it.

I have great passion, conviction, and clarity on the topic of fathers and daughters. Some of these strong feelings have come simply from being the dad of a beautiful daughter who sparked intuitive thoughts and actions over the years. In other words, some of it came naturally. However, many of my thoughts, feelings, and convictions come from my experience as a Young Life leader. I have served in Young Life, a non-denominational, Christian outreach, for all of my adult life. In my time there, I've seen into the lives of thousands of girls and entered into many of their stories. As a male Young Life leader, the focus of my ministry has been the high school guys. However, since Young Life is a co-ed ministry, over the years I've known many girls and have heard many of their stories from our female leaders. My heart breaks over their stories of abuse, abandonment, and neglect. I have seen firsthand the devastating effects of an absent or pathetic dad in the life of a young girl. I have seen their pain, heard their stories, and observed their poor choices as a result of having ineffective or absent fathers. I have come to believe that there may be no more important relationship in the world than that of a father with his daughter. I hope the following pages will serve as a wake-up call to disengaged dads, a road map to hopeful fathers and a confirmation to well-intentioned and intuitive dads who are already on the right path.

Why This Book Now?

I came away from my recent Young Life summer camp assignment urged by an internal voice to finally organize and record my thoughts on this topic. I ended that summer certain that there was something worth discussing and more convinced than ever that the need for this conversation is growing, not shrinking. At camp, I had the opportunity to share for ten minutes in a seminar about girls' worth and value. My friend and fellow Young Life staff member,

Kristy Fox, led a phenomenal "girls only" meeting and she let me share a man's perspective as a small portion. Week after week, I was overwhelmed and surprised by the emotional reaction from the room full of young girls as we discussed the kind of father they deserved, as well as the kind of father God wants to be for them. My input, which I believed to be basic, struck a nerve for many of them. My message was impromptu and somewhat unorganized, yet it seemed to be life-giving for many of the young girls in the audience. Their reaction prompted me to write this book. When camp ended, I received the following feedback from female staff:

"The girl talk with Alan was described by one girl as the most impactful part of camp. She has two absent fathers and said she really needed to hear what was said."

"The talk from Alan at the girls' time was LIFE-CHANGING for a few of my girls. Thank you!"

Kristy Fox had led the seminar for several years without me and had heard things like that many times. Her content was already powerful, but until this point, it had been delivered without a man's perspective. Adding a voice from a male figure seemed to make an even bigger impact than usual.

Wow! I wasn't sure if I should be encouraged or saddened by their feedback. I couldn't believe the effect that my words apparently had on a room of young ladies ages 15-18. That feedback was the catalyst I needed to organize my thoughts and record them here. Kristy's entire seminar is recorded in Chapter 4, and my contribution is in Chapter 5.

Their feedback, as I said, made me realize that this book demands to be written. Even though I hadn't presented my thoughts all that well in my own estimation, who am I to question the impact they made on the girls? And if I have some content that can help young girls and make a big difference for them—if I have some thoughts that may even be "life-changing"—then who am I to withhold them from others? It is more than my own experience, however, that has compelled me to write this book. There is a mountain of experience shared by trusted friends that motivates me as well.

My friend Jaimee, an all-star female Young Life leader, lays it out so eloquently when she speaks of the importance of dads in the lives of girls:

> We were created to be loved. No one but God alone has the opportunity to bestow this type of bonding love, more than a father. The word "daughter" carries an intrinsic message of belonging. It is a signature of love and a word of commitment that binds a girl together at the core of her identity. Who a girl is and who she becomes rests in large part on her place of belonging in her father's life. Our place as Christ's daughters is perhaps one of our most precious relationships in the entire world. It is a place of intimacy and vulnerability with our Father that allows deep roots of trust to form. The adoration and involvement of our earthly father in our lives holds great weight in the formation of our heart, because it ultimately shapes our pursuits in life and our perception of Christ's fatherly love toward us.

It is a father's most precious gift to bestow love upon his daughter. We are all born with an insatiable desire to belong. The presence of a father soothes that longing and gives value and place to the wandering heart of his child. The craving to belong leads girls down many unhealthy paths, and the absence of a father figure or the presence of an abusive father is a catalyst for a deep, dark brokenness that can haunt a girl her entire life.

To his daughter, a father should represent fierce protection, passionate adoration, unconditional commitment and support, and a firm yet gentle source of direction and discernment that will be a voice of guidance her whole life through.

Without a dad to fill this hole, girls often seek after the sense of belonging in all the wrong places. Those whose fathers have left them or neglected them often find themselves bound to a lifelong pursuit to be valued in the eyes of a man. This treacherous path leads to long lines of shallow men looking for a good time who will break and abuse that dream of belonging.

One of my other dear friends shares a painful childhood experience with her father. She sets the stage for us as we further examine the critical importance of a healthy dad in the life of a little girl:

5

The son of poor sharecroppers, my father only graduated from sixth grade and spent his childhood picking cotton. As a child, he was fed a daily diet of fear and shame and grew up to become a man filled with self-contempt. He did the best that he could do to deal with his pain, which, when I was a child, meant he drank a lot of alcohol. And it blurred his vision and slurred his speech and made it difficult for him to contain his self-contempt.

Here's my first memory of my father spilling his self-contempt into the little container of my soul: I was five years old, and I had one of those glorious moments of childhood when you call out to the grownups, "Look at me! Look at me! Aren't I amazing?" I offered my little, authentic self and said to my dad, "Watch me! Daddy, watch me!"

But my father had blurred vision, and he couldn't see how amazing I was in that moment. Instead of celebrating me, he cursed me. He said, in so many slurred words, he wished that I were dead.

I offered him my little, authentic self, and he cursed it.

My life changed significantly in that moment. My course was set. Somehow, in my five-year old heart, I made a vow. I would become invisible. I would learn to hide. I would never call attention to myself, because someone might want me dead.

Another one of my favorite people in the world opens up on the topic of childhood and her dad. She shared with me the following:

My 'true self' was murdered by my alcoholic father. Through many years of hurt, pain, and humiliation, I began to build massive walls, as my 'false self' was constructed as a coping mechanism. My entire childhood was filled with massive dysfunction, and many of my memories have been blocked out as a result. In fact, now as an adult, I cannot even remember birthdays and holidays from my childhood, because my entire childhood was filled with pain.

The performance-oriented thought process I had adopted was obviously not working, so I gave up. It was at this time I joined the party crowd and a promiscuous lifestyle began. My motto with boys became, 'You won't hurt me. I will hurt you.' Often, sex was part of a relationship, but often it became a tool and a power trip. The party life with boys and male attention became a game to me as I continued to operate out of the false self I had constructed due to the horrific dad in my life. I continued to live my life by never letting anyone in, and always seeking male approval due the lack of a father in my life.

Beth, a stellar Young Life leader, forwarded this text to me from her teenage friend "B." It further highlights the importance of a healthy father/daughter relationship.

Having a mostly absent father caused me to get depressed because I thought he didn't love me. I feel needy for attention from a guy because of it.

Ann Shackelton, Marriage and Family Therapist and Senior Vice President of Young Life's HR department adds some important professional insights to this conversation:

Girls are created, different than boys, to admire their fathers. Girls are made to be adored by their fathers and to adore their fathers. Their hearts are shaped for this and there is no replacing it.

This is the primary lens they can see God the Father through. Without a dad, God is distant and absent. Girls see God the way they see their dad. If a girl has a disinterested dad, she will sense that God is disinterested in her. If a girl senses their dad is disappointed in them, they will sense that God is also disappointed in them.

Wow, this is such an important topic! Let's take some time to investigate the issues at hand. Productive lives are hanging in the balance, and broken hearts are yearning for healing. Yet there is good news. There is hope and there is help. Even Hollywood has something positive to contribute on occasion!

Recently, I saw the movie *Battleship*, in which the young misfit hero, Hopper, was about to be kicked out of the Navy. As the plot unfolded, he became romantically involved with the daughter of the

Admiral, who was played by Liam Neeson. As usual, Liam Neeson's character was somewhat tough and intimidating. Hopper spent much of the movie looking for an opportunity to ask the Admiral permission to marry his daughter. Naturally, he was scared and hesitant throughout.

As it turned out, Hopper rose to the challenge to defeat an alien attack force that waged war and attempted to take over planet Earth. He showed incredible courage, wisdom, and strength in the process. He risked his own life in order to save mankind, and he accomplished "Hollywood level" success.

When the movie was all but over, and Hopper had defeated the aliens, he finally had the chance to ask the Admiral for his daughter's hand in marriage. Hopper approached the Admiral, told him that he loved his daughter, and requested permission to marry her. But the Admiral responded with an adamant, "No!"

Hopper replied, "But I just saved the world!"

The Admiral's response is one of my new favorite movie lines of all time. I love his answer, because I resonated with his response. Liam Neeson's character said to his frightened would-be son-in-law, "Saving the world is one thing, Mr. Hopper. My daughter is quite another."

Yes! In other words, "That's right, son. Thanks for saving the world and all, but that does not give you entrance into my daughter's life. It's not that easy. We are talking about my daughter here, and she is more precious to me than the entire world. You saved the world?

It's going to take a lot more than that! I am her sworn protector and defender. She is my treasure."

Many dads I know would say the same thing, or at least think it. Sadly, though, words like these never enter the minds or hearts of so many dads. In the pages to come, we will discuss this problem, look at the effects of disengaged dads, as well as at the outside pressures our society has placed on our girls.

It's my prayer that something in this book will leap out at you and that you will find something helpful and inspiring within. I hope that a light goes on for at least one dad, and that at least one father/daughter relationship is better for it!

To bring this book to you, I collaborated with dozens of people, each of whom has a unique view and experience on this topic. The pages of this book contain real life examples of the "state of our girls," coming directly from those with an authentic, front-row seat. We will examine the current state of affairs in our culture and see what effect it is having on our girls as well. Additionally, you will hear from dads who have run this race, raised great daughters, and "done it right"—or at least, mostly right. It should be noted that no one is claiming perfection, either in themselves or in their daughters. I will bring a number of field-tested experiences for you to examine, use and even improve upon.

Perhaps the most powerful content of all will come directly from girls who have been loved well and are now old enough to appreciate their dads and the great relationship they have. They recognize that most girls don't have what they have. You will hear directly from them about what their dads did right and the profound impact it had on them through adolescence and into adulthood. We will also hear from Kristy Fox, as she lays out the particulars of her "girls only" seminar—a seminar she created that has been greatly impactful for many years.

Dads with daughters, I pray that your relationships with your daughters will never be the same. It is my hope that, as men, we will think of our girls differently and become more aware of the assault that our society levels upon them. God bless you as you delve into this important topic. May you be a better dad, husband, youth leader, or friend because of it. Welcome to my journey as a dad with a daughter, and God bless you in yours!

Real Talk

"When a girl begins to hear and learn who God is, she almost always associates her father with a picture of who God is. I spend a lot of time talking through the fact that as humans we fail, but our heavenly Father never fails. If a girl hasn't experienced tangible love and investment from her dad (touch, affirmation, value, unconditional support, discipline), then it's really hard for her to trust in the love of God."

"I watched a movie the other day, in which a teenage boy said, "It's the worst" when dads try too hard. A teenge girl looked at him and said, "No, what would be worse is if they didn't try at all."

Chapter 2

The Grand Slam of Input

My Journey to Perspective, Insight, and Conviction

In sports, a "grand slam" incorporates a four-part victory. In baseball, a grand slam is hitting a homerun with the bases loaded, meaning the runner scores four runs on one swing of the bat. In other sports like golf and tennis, a grand slam means winning each of the four major tournaments in the sport. Grand slams in any sport are very hard to accomplish, relatively rare, and always a big deal.

In 1991, I was hit with a grand slam of my own that shaped my early years of being a dad with a daughter. I call it the "Grand Slam of Input." Over the course of a year, four distinct and eye-opening conversations set the stage and sparked a thought process that has shaped the rest of my life. All four occurrences were unrelated and disconnected from one another. They all came from different perspectives, yet all four spoke clearly on the topic of father/daughter relationships. Or more accurately, on how a father should think and what a father should do. I came away from this Grand Slam of Input with a firm and clear resolution. It wasn't something I said aloud, but it was as clear a thought as I have ever had. Never before had I made a more firm resolution. But before I tell you my resolution, let me tell you about the Grand Slam.

I look back at that year—1991—as a gift from the Lord and the most formative year of my life. That year sent me down a path of insight, conviction, and actions that changed my life and further shaped my role as a young dad who happened to be blessed with a little girl. As a guy who grew up in a family with all boys, I'd never even thought about raising a daughter, let alone had the opportunity to gain any experience or wisdom along the way by seeing it done. It was never modeled or discussed. I started my life as a dad with a daughter at ground zero, and I'm eternally grateful for 1991, and the "Grand Slam of Input" I received.

A Word About Young Life

First, let me give you a brief background on the ministry of Young Life, because Young Life is the common denominator among all four elements in my "Grand Slam of Input." As previously mentioned, I have served as a Young Life volunteer or staff member my entire adult life. As a high school student, I was invited to a Young Life club at Leland High School in San Jose, California, in 1980. My involvement with Young Life changed my life, because it introduced me to a relationship with Jesus Christ. In those years at my school, Young Life was big and fun, and it seemed as though everyone attended the club. All my friends were in Young Life and it wasn't long until I joined in. Young Life is a Christ-centered, non-denominational outreach to all kinds of kids everywhere: high school, junior high and college kids. We serve kids in the suburbs, kids in the city, kids from all kinds of cultures from all around the world, kids with disabilities and teen moms. The mission statement of Young Life is: "Introducing adolescents to Jesus Christ and helping them grow in their faith." Young Life's core methodology is pursuing kids through personal relationships and its focus is that of disinterested kids who do not have an experience in the Christian faith. Young Life values humor, adventure, and excellence as they pursue lost kids. For more information on Young Life, visit www.younglife.org.

When I finished high school, I knew one thing for sure. I knew that I was going to stay involved with Young Life in one way or the other. Immediately, I entered freshman leadership training and was placed on a team of leaders to start a Young Life club in the spring of 1982. After nine years of volunteer leadership, I felt God calling me on staff, and I entered Young Life vocationally in 1991. I am grateful for this path, because it was through the community of Young Life that I gained the insight I needed to shape me as a father with a daughter. It was in this context that I was hit with the "Grand Slam of Input," through four specific and life-changing conversations.

Conversation #1

I credit life-altering Conversation #1 to Rick Hendrick. Rick was a mentor and a friend who shared my love and commitment to Young Life. As I built a relationship with Rick, we often met for breakfast or lunch to get to know one another. Over the course of several months of sharing life over bacon and eggs, we discussed our daughters. (Rick has two children—one son and one daughter.) One of these meals became the setting for the first of four life-altering conversations that paved the way for my life as a dad with a daughter. At the time, my daughter Brittany was only three, and Rick's daughter had graduated high school. He was obviously further down this road than I was. At some point, the subject of boys entered into our discussion. I'd later learn that the topic of boys often enters the conversations between dads with daughters. Fear of the young male moving in on our daughters is a common denominator we all share, because we were all young males once and so were our friends. We know too much! But I digress . . . .

Rick shared with me some struggles over a particular boyfriend that had been hanging around his daughter. Apparently, the boy was acting a bit flippant and careless in his conversations about his daughter and the boy was obviously not communicating the level of care and concern that Rick desired. It's every dad's nightmare: a young boy for whom his daughter has fallen, who does not value his daughter enough. (More on that in Chapter 5.)

Rick relayed to me the essence of a conversation he had with the young suitor. As Rick tactfully expressed his desire for the boy to show a greater level of care toward his daughter, the boy failed to rise up, and continued his flippant and cavalier attitude toward their relationship. "Chill out," he seemed to be telling Rick. "We're fine, and it will all work out. Don't worry." Rick's frustration grew, because the last thing a caring dad wants to hear from his daughter's boyfriend is, "Chill out." Most dads I know are anything but "chill" toward their daughters. We are protective . . . . even overly protective. A dad wants his daughter's boyfriend to communicate in a reassuring and respectful manner, but that was not happening for Rick. Exasperated, Rick interrupted the boy with a clear and concise statement that became "Conversation #1" in my Grand Slam of Input. His words grabbed my attention, resonated with me immediately, and stopped the disrespectful boy mid-sentence.

Rick said, **"Hey, you have to understand something here. My daughter is my PRIZED POSSESSION."**

"Yes!" I thought. "Exactly! Of course! I deeply agree!" Being in full-time ministry, we have always lived modestly and have been content in doing so. In the world's eyes, I have never been considered wealthy, but I do feel like a rich man. So when Rick told the boy that his daughter was his "prized possession," I loved it. I agree, because my daughter, Brittany, was and is my prized possession, too. When I think of the word "possession," I do not think of it as an inappropriate, overbearing, "possessive" ownership that isn't healthy. Rather, I think of possession in a loving, protective way that defines my place and role in Brittany's life, and hers in mine. "Prized Possession" is one that I hold above all else and cherish with all of my heart. It's a treasure with deep, intrinsic value. After all, Brittany is "mine," because God saw fit to entrust her to me as her dad. She is my responsibility and my daughter, and I would defend and protect her to the death. I'm so grateful for Rick's phrase, because it captured my thoughts and feelings for my daughter, and it fueled my direction as a father in those early years.

As an immediate application after Conversation #1 with Rick, I wanted the three-year-old Brittany Smyth to understand how I felt about her. I wanted her to feel how much I valued her. I grabbed onto this phrase "prized possession" in a practical way. I couldn't wait to get home that day and introduce her to this concept. I knew that

Brittany would be spared a lot of angst the rest of her life if she were clear on the fact that her dad loved and valued her. And so, we began a little game. I taught my daughter a little call-and-response. I'd ask, "What are you?" She'd answer, "Your prized possession!" I'd continue, "And . . . ?" and she'd finish, ". . . don't you forget it!"

This became our "thing," and it continued through the years. I have a cute video of her at age five, reciting that response. In fact, to this day, Brittany still responds, "Your prized possession," any time I prompt, "What are you?" In a brutal world where women are degraded and fathers are absent, my daughter grew up knowing that she was her daddy's "prized possession." She knew that she was more valuable than anything in my life, and that she was cherished above all else.

Hearing and adopting the phrase "Prized Possession" regarding my daughter was the first catalyst conversation in the Grand Slam of Input. I didn't need to be talked into this idea, but it confirmed and put into words what I already felt for Brittany. It was the beginning of a new path, but I didn't sense it as such at the time. Only in hindsight, after three more conversations occurred, did I recognize its impact.

Conversation #2

Significant Conversation #2 in the Grand Slam of Input came in the summer of 1991. As part of my responsibilities as a Young Life staff member, I was required to serve at a Young Life camp for a month during the summer. My particular role in August of 1991 was that of Program Director, which meant I was responsible for all of the entertainment activities that happened at camp—basically, 1,001 things. That summer, I created the overall camp schedule that moved 400 kids in and out of activities and to and from events. I planned everything from logistics to humor. I accounted for supplies, timing, music, flow, and fun. I had to communicate clearly with multiple groups of people in order to pull off the various events that I planned. As is typical for Program Directors, I'd spent six months before our time at camp, planning every detail in every event. I shot videos, had phone calls, made costumes, practiced skits, and purchased supplies.

At the end of all this, each week of camp ends with a "trip leader evaluation." This is a meeting in which the leaders of the various Young Life groups attending camp meet to give their feedback on the week. Typically, this meeting can go one of two directions: sometimes, there is harsh feedback that seems unfair and not very helpful. Sometimes, the meeting leads to helpful critique, which makes the program better for the following weeks. In the summer of '91, though, the evaluation meeting went another direction entirely for me.

In one of those meetings, a statement was made which became catalyst Conversation #2 in the life of Alan Smyth. In this meeting after camp, I received a comment so impactful that it further shaped my role as a dad with a daughter. I entered that meeting with my notepad, ready to hear how to improve our program for students. I assumed there were many things we could do better, and I was a little apprehensive to hear all about them, because I had devoted so much time trying to get all 1,001 things right for this camp.

It was this setting, sitting in the circle waiting for my turn to receive my critique, where I received the next significant piece of the "Grand Slam of Input." Finally, it was my turn. The attention turned to the "Program." Time to hear how I did at camp. "Time to get blasted for not being funny enough, or for having a bad schedule," I thought. Then, one of the female trip leaders had this to say:

"The most significant thing for my girls this week at camp was watching Alan interact with his daughter."

"Wait, what?" I thought. "What did she say?" What about the schedule? What about the humor? What about all the new and creative things we did? What about the fact that we made it snow in August, and orchestrated 40 of Santa's elves to arrive? What about all the planning, and costumes, and great music? We even had Darth Vader make an appearance! My three-year-old daughter was not on the agenda. She was not featured in the program in any way. She did not appear in a skit. She was just a normal, healthy, happy little girl, running around Young Life camp, having fun. I was confused.

I wasn't intentionally lifting up my daughter that week of camp. I was simply trying to be an engaged dad as best as I could in the middle of a hectic schedule. I just squeezed in a few moments with my daughter each day, whenever possible. I remember driving around in a golf cart with Brittany on my lap, and a few moments here and there with her on my shoulders. I had held her hand as we walked down to the pool. All normal stuff, it seemed to me. In my estimation, I hadn't given my daughter enough attention during the week, due to my role as Program Director.

And yet, in the middle of extreme busyness, apparently a bunch of high school girls were extremely impacted by me simply spending time with my daughter. Seeing a dad engaged with his daughter and spending time with her was, apparently, a big deal to the girls at camp. This blew me away. I wanted to hear how great the program was, not what kind of dad I was. While it was not a big deal to me, it seemed to be a big deal to those who were watching. This confirmed to me that I seemed to be on the right path as a father. Sadly, it also confirmed that my actions were not normal to most girls. I was struck by the deep deficit of attention and affection many girls experienced with their own dads. My antenna was now officially up concerning fathers and daughters, because what was "no big deal" and insufficient to me, seemed of great importance and over the top to a bunch of young girls.

Conversation #3

Catalyst Conversation #3 came in the fall of 1991. As part of my Young Life staff responsibilities, I was required to attend various staff trainings and overnights. While I certainly enjoyed the structured part of the meetings, the highlight always came after the meetings, during free time. It was both meaningful and fun to simply hang out with my fellow staffers. Cracking jokes, sharing stories, and discussing life was our usual agenda. Maybe a late-night food run or games would happen, too. One night, during one of these unstructured, relaxed times, I had another significant conversation that further shaped and propelled me down my parenting path. Here, the Grand Slam of Input increased in intensity for me. I credit Jerry Mann, current pastor and longtime Young Life staff member in San Francisco, for hitting me between the eyes with a poignant and frightening comment. To him, it was no big deal. But to me, it stopped me in my tracks and further solidified my desire to be a great dad to my precious little girl.

As we sat around the kitchen table at the house we'd rented, Jerry asked, "Alan, are you loving your daughter?"

"Um, yeah, of course," I responded. "What do you mean?"

He replied, **"Because whatever she doesn't get from you, she will go looking for in other guys."**

Whoa. Ouch. Okay, let me get my mind around this. Are you saying, if I don't love my daughter in a significant way—in a way that she feels and understands—that she will go looking for love in other places? Are you saying that I, as her father, have a direct impact on the choices she will make later on with boyfriends? On who they are, and how often they are around, and even what happens behind closed doors?

Wow. Suddenly, my role as Brittany's dad got bigger and more real than ever before. Not that it didn't seem real already, but it just leapt to another level. It was as though I'd been parenting in black and white, and Jerry's comments made me parent in color. Before, I was playing checkers, but now I learned I was playing chess.

As a Young Life leader, I'd seen many times what needy high school girls looked like. I had watched young girls throw themselves at punk guys who were no more interested in them as humans than they were in flying to the moon. The worst high school guy is one who selfishly looks for conquests to provide bragging rights in the locker room. He obviously isn't looking to settle down and build a life around a family. In the best cases, guys are looking for companionship, and they have good intentions. However, even the best of guys struggle to make great choices. (More on that later in the book) But typically, guys are looking for another notch in their belts.

That day, I decided it was absolutely unacceptable to me that Brittany would be forced to go out looking for love, attention, and affection from some punk because I somehow withheld those things from her. No way was I going to be responsible for sending her down the path I had seen over and over through my duties as a Young Life leader. My marching orders were simple from then on: I would show Brittany love, attention, and affection in a consistent way that she would understand. If I could do this over the next 15 years, she might have a chance at making it through junior high and high school relatively unscathed. My experience as a Young Life leader taught me that she would be entering a shark tank soon enough, and I knew that she needed to enter that world with a high degree of self-confidence and a low degree of neediness. And now, I knew that I had a lot to do with arming her with what she needed as a young girl.

I knew that, in time, Brittany would be mixing with a bunch of needy girls who would pressure her into stooping to their level regarding their views on boys, parties, language, and actions. I knew that soon enough she would be entering a world where needy, selfish, conquering boys would see her more as prey than as the beautiful, precious daughter of God that she actually was. To say that the rest of the world was not going to regard her as their "prized possession" was a colossal understatement. I knew this, intuitively and experientially. Now, thanks to Jerry Mann, I could put the concept into words. As with Rick's "Prized Possession" phrase, I didn't need to be talked into Jerry's words. They resonated with me immediately, and they made sense to me based on everything I already knew. I'd just never heard it in such a clear, concise, and compelling way before: **"What your daughter doesn't get from you, she will go looking for in other guys!"**

Wow. Enough said. I'm on it! Game on! I may not be a rocket scientist, but I can add two plus two. My Grand Slam of Input was really taking shape. Unbeknownst to me at the time, God was speaking to me and shaping who I was as a man and a father. It was now time for catalyst Conversation #4, and the final piece of the Grand Slam of Input that sealed the deal for me and led me to my crystal clear resolution.

Conversation #4

The final piece of the puzzle—Conversation #4—came as I led my club trip to Young Life camp. Every Young Life leader recruits kids to summer camp, and camp is a high point every year. We often say, "It will be the best week of your life, or your money back." We take thousands of kids per week to camps nationwide and internationally. In those years, I was the team leader of my club at Gunderson High School in San Jose. We had a big, fun club where it was not uncommon to have over a 100 kids in attendance each week, and getting kids to summer camp was a huge part of our club strategy.

Not only did kids have more fun than they ever had before, but more importantly, they had an unmistakable encounter with Jesus Christ through the camp program and speaker.

That year, we took a bus full of kids from Gunderson High School. It was a great week with lots of fun and lots of spiritual growth, too. Most significant for me, though, was a two-part conversation I had with girls from our club. On the first night of camp, the speaker led us through a few icebreaker questions. He told us to turn around and make a small circle with the people we were sitting near. Our leaders always sat right in the middle of the kids we brought to camp, so my circle turned out to be kids from our club, who I already knew pretty well. The speaker asked a few questions from stage: "What are you looking forward to at camp this week?" and "Where are you from?" But the next two questions caught my attention and played a huge role in the Grand Slam of Input. The speaker asked, "What is the hardest thing about your family?" Every girl in my circle answered the same:

"My relationship with my dad."

The final question was, "What is the thing you would most like to change about your life?" Again, every girl responded the same:

"My relationship with my dad."

Their responses were huge for me. Again, before Brittany's birth, I'd had no hands-on experience with girls—not with my daughter, or anyone's daughter. Hearing this answer from the girls I knew from my

Young Life club broke my heart. Every girl in my circle that night was hurting because of the relationship they had with their dads.

This realization occupied my thoughts for the rest of the week. I cared about these girls, but more than that, I cared about my own little girl. I decided that I needed more information, and so, on the bus ride home, I probed a little deeper. I reminded the girls of the answers they had given that night. I told them that I wanted to make sure I had a great relationship with my daughter in 15 years. I asked them what I needed to do.

None of them had a horrific story of an abusive dad, like we often hear about. But, all of them told the story of a busy dad who had disengaged years before. They told of dads who had basically given up and abdicated their active role in their lives. I got the impression that their dads were not knuckleheads, but rather just guys who had gotten busy with life and career and simply did not have time for their daughters anymore. I am guessing that, as their daughters grew older, these dads wrongly assumed that their voice and role was not as important anymore. Now that their daughters were turning into young ladies, they somehow thought their wives' input was more necessary than their own. On the contrary, I would argue that while a mom's guidance and input is invaluable, a dad's relationship through these adolescent years is absolutely critical.

The girls on the bus thought it was "cute" that I was drilling them with questions about fatherhood, so they indulged me further. They gave me advice that I've never forgotten. They acknowledged that they hadn't always made things easy on their dads. They told stories of blowing off their dads and treating them disrespectfully. There were many times, I'm sure, when these girls were moody and emotional. After acknowledging all of this and naming their part in the situation, the girls offered this sound advice: **"Don't give up!" they said. "Don't let Brittany push you away."**

The girls encouraged me to fight through the hard times, and they explained that, regardless of what she might say or do, a daughter really wants and needs her dad in her life. Their advice was the fuel I needed as Brittany grew up.

There it is—the Grand Slam of Input that shaped and propelled me into a certain way of thinking and acting as a father in the years to follow. These four conversations solidified a paradigm for me, and acted as a catalyst for thought.

Over the course of a year, I resonated with the fact that Brittany was indeed my Prized Possession. I began to understand that my "normal" interactions with my daughter were not normal to other girls, and therefore this whole topic must be a big deal. My system was shocked with the realization that "what Brittany doesn't get from me, she will go looking for in other guys." And I learned from the girls I knew that daughters desperately want relationships with their dads. All four were incredibly powerful concepts that I took with me, internalized, and lived out to the best of my ability for years to come.

And another crucial insight: Don't give up! I resolved to stay the course, and to keep pushing even if the road ahead grew rocky. After all, "Don't give up!" means that the end goal is worthwhile. I certainly felt strongly that helping my daughter make it through life in a healthy way, and having a great relationship with her along the way, was indeed worthwhile!

The Grand Slam of Input led me to the powerful resolution that I mentioned earlier in this chapter. As clearly and powerfully as I had ever thought, the following resolution became my internal mantra, and it guided my parenting of Brittany through her growing years. My resolution:

> **I will do everything within my power to give Brittany all the resources, love, affection and attention she needs to make good and life-giving choices in her life. Should Brittany end up making some poor choices later in her life, it will not be because her dad wasn't involved with her or didn't love her well.**

It was one of the few things I could actually control. Of course, I can't prevent her from making poor choices, and I can't control her or her decision-making process. In fact, there was much more out of my control than actually in my control. However, I could control my interaction with my daughter. I could control whether or not I spent regular and consistent time with her. I could control the kind of input that I gave Brittany. I could control whether or not I gave up if things got hard. A young girl's choices, I was learning, are very connected to her relationship with her dad. It isn't the only factor, but it's an important factor. So I resolved that if Brittany chose a hard road to go down in life, she could not say it was because I was disengaged from her. I determined that I would do everything within my power so that

Brittany would not sit at a Young Life camp in 15 years and tell her leader that her dad was absent. I resolved that I would do everything within my power so that Brittany would never say, "The hardest thing about my family is my relationship with my dad."

Real Talk

"As society and culture takes its toll on girls today, girls begin to lose a sense of their own value. It's a painful loss and often leads to a search for painkillers. Alcohol and drugs are often used to numb the pain. Girls compromise their God-given value to meet the expectations of boys who can't possibly understand the beautiful treasures God has created them to be. "If I only give my boyfriend what he wants," they think, "then I'll matter. I'll be something, I'll belong." The problem is, such a pattern reduces a girl to her ability to perform and her willingness to have sex. Such a degradation of her identity will act as a huge wall against her understanding of who God has created her to be and the value He, as her Father, has placed on her life."

Chapter 3

The Assault on Our Girls, and the Realities of Their Environment

I said it: there is an assault on our young women, and it's even worse than I once thought. In fact, the assault begins long before we even call them "women." The safety of childhood is shrinking ever smaller, and young girls are being forced to grow up in a dangerous setting.

In her book, *Reviving Ophelia*, Mary Pipher, Ph.D. writes, "Girls today are much more oppressed. They are coming of age in a more dangerous, sexualized, and media-saturated culture. They face incredible pressures to be beautiful and sophisticated, which in junior high means using chemicals and being sexual." Pipher goes on to say that, "America today limits girls' development, truncates their wholeness, and leaves many of them traumatized."

This chapter—and this entire book—isn't intended to deliver a lot of stats or refer to countless studies on the father/daughter relationships. I'm not trying to prove a point as much as shine a light on this important topic to create awareness. I hope to prompt a deeper thought process for those who are involved with young girls, either as dads or youth workers. There are plenty of stats, figures, and studies readily available, if you are interested. But from a broader perspective, we know that the last two decades have seen a dramatic increase in alarming categories. Issues such as eating disorders, alcoholism, sexual and physical assaults, sexually transmitted diseases, self-inflicted injuries, and suicide are at all-time highs. You might think that this chapter does not really apply to you if you are an engaged dad, already doing a great job raising your daughter. (She will thank you for that someday.) Yet, while it may be true that the issues discussed here do not directly affect your daughter, she is absolutely growing up in this culture, and many of her friends are being chewed up in the process. The pressures spoken about in this chapter are all around her, and whether you like it or not, your daughter is affected.

Much of the media, including popular music, has launched a full-scale war on our girls, although I'm sure they don't view it as such. To the industry, it's just good business. As a father with a daughter, my heart breaks for the culture in which she has grown up. I have spent much of my daughter's life building her up, honoring her as God's precious masterpiece, and treating her like a princess. The problem is, I'm outgunned! The multi-billion dollar entertainment industry has spent far more resources, time, and energy in tearing her down, objectifying her, and referring to her as garbage. Today, our girls are seen as sexual, disposable objects. From magazines and billboards to commercials, movies, and songs, women's bodies are being exploited and sexualized. They are marketed to sell toothpaste, hamburgers, and everything in between.

Pipher continues, "Something new is happening. Adolescence has always been hard, but it's harder now because of cultural changes in the last decade."

Let's take a brief look at three realities pressuring our girls.

The Reality of the Media and Entertainment

One reality for our girls is that they are lacking healthy, wholesome role models in our media. There are some great young girls out there in the entertainment industry, but most of the ones making good choices stay out of the public eye. They don't make very good "news," because they don't get into trouble and land themselves on the front page of the tabloids. The role models who do sell news are in and out of rehab, jail and marriages. From these "role models," our girls learn at least eight destructive lessons:

1. You must be beautiful at all costs.
2. If you are beautiful, you will gain attention.
3. Drugs and alcohol are normal.
4. Having promiscuous sex is acceptable.
5. Going in and out of drug rehab is a part of life.
6. Expect a cavalier, temporary approach to marriage.
7. Money buys fame and friends.
8. Dressing immodestly is expected and will gain you attention.

These lessons are delivered daily on the doorsteps of our girls' lives through the tabloids, television, music and the movies. Unless parents—and especially fathers—offer a different message, our girls are left at the mercy of the media's version of beauty, health and success. And the media is driven by the dollar. The well-being of our daughters is not the media's main concern. The bottom line is the bottom line, regardless of the toll it takes on our young women. The media pulls out all stops and uses every trick at its disposal to seduce our daughters.

You and I know the power of technology and medical procedures. The power of an airbrushed photo and surgical enhancement is significant. But our girls are not always so aware of the manufactured nature of what they see. As a result, they hold themselves to a standard they cannot possibly achieve and are often sent down a tragic path that often ends in destruction. This first "assault" is a bit sneaky and deceptive. In some ways, it is almost subliminal. In essence, it comes through the back door and sneaks up on our girls. Consider this quote, which sums up the goals and strategies of much of the multi-billion dollar popular media machine:

> "If you can get their emotions going—make them forget their logic—you've got them. At MTV, we don't shoot for the 14-year-olds. We own them."—Bob Pittman, creator of MTV

It's frightening to know that MTV's goal is the "ownership" of our kids. Sadly, they have accomplished their goals in far too many. Many of our kids receive far more input from sources like MTV than they do from an engaged parent who wants the very best for them.

The results of the insidious actions of the media machine and some segments of the entertainment industry are starting to be seen at an alarmingly young age. The American Psychological Association set up a task force on the "Sexualization of Girls," as a response to public concern that it's an increasing problem. Published online in the journal *Sex Roles*, a new study confirms these concerns, finding that "girls as young as six years old want to be sexy."

"It's very possible that girls wanted to look like the sexy doll because they believe sexiness leads to popularity, which comes with many social advantages," says lead researcher Christy Starr.

Whatever happened to being a kid? Where is childhood going? Our kids are being stolen from us, and our daughters are being assaulted right in front of our eyes.

The Reality of Popular Music

I wish I had purchased Apple stock 15 years ago, and lots of it! Apple has experienced meteoric success over the last decade due to the efforts, genius, and technological breakthroughs they have enjoyed. I remember the first time I heard about a new product called an "iPod." My friend explained that this little device could hold a thousand songs. I was flabbergasted. "You have to be kidding!" I thought. "How do they do that?" Of course, we're all aware of the wildfire-like sales that this device has experienced. In April of 2007, Apple had already sold 100 million iPods. A year later, in April 2008, they had sold 152 million iPods. And in 2011, according to Apple, that number had more than doubled to over 321 million iPods.

It's simply staggering to think about how many kids have iPods plugged into their ears.

This invention has transformed the way users interact with the music industry. Music is now easier, cheaper and quicker to get than ever before. With multiple music downloading and sharing sites (both authorized and unauthorized), not to mention the ability to swap and trade music among people, there is an almost endless capability for kids to own and listen to any music they want. I don't think I know anyone who doesn't own an iPod or who at least listens to music digitally in some way. On a junior high or high school campus, countless numbers of kids walk from class to class with earphones plugged in and playing all day long.

So what's the problem? The problem is, popular music, including the hip hop/rap culture, has launched a disgusting attack on our adolescent girls and boys. We have rewarded artists whose lyrics are disgusting, degrading, and attacking to our young girls. We've made them rich and famous and empowered them to keep feeding our kids garbage. Our kids spend hours a day with destructive words and concepts blasting in their ears and into their brains. Kids are desensitized to the vulgar and profane and they learn through repetition extremely dangerous lessons that affect their attitudes and perceptions.

And, even if this doesn't describe your daughter, it describes most of the kids your daughter comes in contact with every day—which means is still affects your daughter. Our young boys are being trained to think this is the proper way to treat a woman, and our young girls are being told that it must be okay, because those producing this filth are wildly successful in the world's eyes.

One of the biggest influences when it comes to downgrading women's dignity is the lyrics from thousands of chart-topping hits. These words are dirty and vulgar in the way they reference women.

Don't take my word for it. The lyrics from these popular "artists" speak for themselves. Know that the writers, producers, and singers of these words have made billions of dollars because of them. Remember that our boys and girls are hearing and internalizing this content. They are being trained in how to think about themselves and how to treat others. I encourage you to do a "Google" search and you can make up your own mind.

Please put down this book right now and turn on your computer. In an effort to keep this book "PG," I will not reproduce these lyrics here, but let you see for your self. Warning: The lyrics may be—should be!—extremely offensive. Those readers who are more sensitive to the rawness at hand may prefer to skip the computer search, and take my word for it. But, to truly experience the reality of what is out there, please proceed with my dircections.

For starters, search for song lyrics from a few of the following artists: "Lil Wayne," "Eminem," "Dr. Dre," "Snoop Dog," "Ludacris," "Cadillac Don," "Akon," "Ghostface Killah," "Ja Rule," "Drake," and "Jay Z." If you are feeling particularly brave, go ahead and Google the phrase "degrading songs about women" and see what comes up. Know that all of this filth comes from prominent hip hop/rap artists in the marketplace right now. I am not sharing this for shock value. This is the new normal for what is available and popular. I'm sorry to immerse you in this toxic river of degradation, but not as sorry as I am that our kids swim in this polluted water every day.

These lyrics, and others like them, are pumping through the earphones, car stereos, and locker rooms of a huge majority of our kids. And coming from a parent, I would not rule out the possibility that some of this music has made its way onto your child's iPod. My advice: physically inspect your kids' iPod for music that you deem as inappropriate. This is just a small sampling to give you the idea. The artists who produce these songs have become incredibly wealthy, so our society rewards this behavior. Therefore, kids assume it must be acceptable and appropriate. Our young boys are being trained to think that girls are no more than "things" that exist solely for their use and pleasure. In fact, by reading some of those lyrics, one would think that girls are no better than human garbage. This is the environment in which our kids are growing up.

A recent Rand Corp. study says:

> The more often teens listen to sexually degrading songs marked by obscenities and stereotypes of women as sex objects and men as sexual predators, the likelier they are to have sex at an early age. A sex drive is, of course, a natural thing for adolescents, the study notes, but engaging in intercourse too early can lead to unwanted pregnancies and sexually transmitted diseases, or STDs, making the matter a public health concern.

Despite renewed calls for a ban on lyrics that degrade women, big record companies have little incentive to stop producing lurid chart-topping rap tunes that rake in billions of dollars. "Throw Some D's" by Rich Boy was at No. 3 on Billboard's rap chart, and has a chorus that hits all the lows in its references to black men, women, and sex. Produced by SRC/Universal, Rich Boy sold 224,000 albums, and his popular single was downloaded 381,000 times in the first six weeks it was available. Young Jeezy, another SRC/Universal artist, released his last album last December, and sold one million copies. The single "Go Getta," downloaded 315,000 times, contains a raunchy reference to female genitalia.

The explosion of the Internet and the extreme ease of downloading and sharing music have further complicated the problem. Considering that the absent father problem is not limited to only girls, and our young boys are missing their dads, too, the stage is being set for a combustible situation. In the past, when my son had inappropriate music, I'd break the CD and give him a handful of pieces. Then, I would talk to him about why the music was unacceptable and would not be allowed in our home, on his iPod, or in his car. My son was a good kid who made good choices, but this music can show up on a CD without even looking for it, through an innocent music swap with a friend. My son and I had that conversation more than once as he grew up, but most young boys don't have engaged dads looking for and acting on this content.

A lot of great dads out there are simply ignorant to the brutally vulgar lyrics that their sons are listening to on their iPods right now. The acquisition and transfer of music happens so quickly and easily these days that it is almost impossible to keep up with, even for a vigilant dad who is on top of it. The polluted rivers of television, movies, media and music are pouring into the culture that surrounds our kids. As a result, our sons and daughters are swimming in an ocean full of toxic waste from which it is hard to escape.

The Reality for Our Young Boys

This book is focusing on our daughters, but we need to take a moment and acknowledge the impact on our sons's. Droves of young boys are left without engaged dads, just like young girls. The specific effects may be different, but reality is the same. When a dad is missing from the life of a young male, he is left without a strong male voice of accountability and guidance. He is left with a huge void of leadership that is easily filled by all the outside voices. Many heroic single moms do the best they can, but they are often overwhelmed with all that they have to juggle. Even the best, strongest, and most engaged mom does not have a male experience or voice to speak from. Our young boys without a strong male voice in their lives will struggle and be deficient at some level. Often, as the young male grows, he is on his own to determine how to be a man in a brutal culture. In many ways, he is being raised by the countless "reality" shows and ruthless marketing machines like MTV. Our young boys are targets for the music artists who produce their vile product. Our young boys take in some of the most disgusting, degrading and destructive song lyrics imaginable on a regular basis.

So, why do I even mention boys in a book about the state of our girls? Besides the fact that we need to be deeply concerned about our young men, guys are also a major part of the tumultuous environment in which our girls are forced to live. A society full of undisciplined, unhealthy boys who have been raised with insufficient accountability and guidance plays a huge role in how our girls are treated, talked about, and acted upon. A young girl can be deeply scarred by either the malicious intent or the careless mistake of the many guys she interacts with every single day. The male population, both young and old, is very much one of the obstacles and realities that our girls must deal with.

When our young boys are left to figure out appropriate roles on their own, sadly, many of them fail miserably. This impacts our girls, because so many of them are longing for male attention due to their absent fathers. Many are willing to give themselves to the first male figure that pays attention to them. Many of our young boys have been strongly influenced by the hip hop/rap scene, and thus are out looking for a vulnerable female, because they intend to live out their training in real life. More than ever, girls are at risk, and more than ever, boys are primed to take advantage of them.

Undoubtedly, all of these pressures have a negative effect on our girls. It fires me up that while I spent my daughter's lifetime telling her she was beautiful, our society spent the same amount of time (and billions of dollars in marketing monies) telling her she wasn't. Our girls go through life carrying unrealistic expectations and pressures weighing them down like a backpack full of boulders. The pressure is growing, and many of our girls are falling beneath the weight.

In 2011, Dove® released the findings of its largest global study to date on women's relationship with beauty, "The Real Truth About Beauty: Revisited." The study revealed that only 4 percent of women around the world consider themselves beautiful and that anxiety about looks begins at an early age. In a study of over 1,200 10 to 17 year olds, a majority of girls, 72 percent, said they felt tremendous pressure to be beautiful. The study also found that only 11 percent of girls around the world feel comfortable using the word beautiful to describe their looks, showing that there is a universal increase in beauty pressure, and a decrease in girls' confidence as they grow older.

Regrettably, this chapter could go on much longer because there is an endless amount of material on this subject. Suffice it to say, our kids are under attack by our society. I am not on a crusade against music or boys. It would not be enough for someone to simply say, "Okay, we are not allowing music." First, it wouldn't work. It's everywhere, and too accessible. More importantly, the music is not the problem. It is only a symptom of the problem. The real issue is that our society has decayed to the point where music like this is even possible. It is much bigger than any song or artist producing it. The mainstream media, along with popular music, is waging war on healthy values and actions. Our girls are being assaulted every day, and many are crumbling under the attack. Many more will suffer painful results in their lives because of their reaction to the circumstances around them. As a dad or youth worker, you can either engage in the battle or go on pretending that it's not that bad. I say, let's mount up, fasten our armor, and enter the battle! Our little girls (and boys) are hanging in the balance. It's time for engagement and vigilance in the environment around our kids. They need protectors and defenders. They need a strong alternative voice in their lives on a regular basis. It's not someone else's job. It's our job. Dads, don't run from your duties!

As we close this chapter, you may be thinking, "That was depressing." I agree. But more depressing still would be an entire generation of fathers failing to fight for their sons and daughters in this battle. Ignorance is not bliss. Ignorance, in this case, is defeat. But don't lose heart. There are some extremely encouraging, positive and helpful chapters still to come. We can fight the good fight and win if we keep arming ourselves with good information, determination and good strategy. That's what lies ahead, so keep reading!

Real Talk

"My dad is lazy and absent from my life. Although he is home, he sits around watching TV or doing other things rather than spend time with our family. He only communicates with me when he is mad at me for something I have done. When he knows he has done something that upsets my brother or me, he tries to buy our love back by getting us presents. He gave me a gift a few months ago that is still sitting in my closet. It's still wrapped, because I don't even care enough to open it. I can't even look at it because it makes me so angry."

Chapter 4

Kristy's Seminar

This chapter is written by Kristy Fox, a 20-year veteran of the Young Life staff in Southern California. Kristy shares the story of how her seminar for girls came into being, as well as its content.

For years, my heart has ached for teenage girls. As I have watched, listened to, interacted with, befriended and walked alongside teenage young women the past 20 years, that ache only continues to increase. As adults, we hear how hard it is to be a teenager in today's world, but as you bend your ear to listen to the hearts and thoughts of these young girls, you really see what it means. It isn't just the external pressures around them that make life difficult, but it's also the internal pressure and negative self-talk that comes from within.

Our girls face pressure to succeed, to excel, to have the right curves in the right places, to be skinny, to be fun, to be pretty, to be sexy, to be athletic, to be feminine, to be "enough." The teenage world in which they live is exhausting and impossible, and it leaves countless girls believing they aren't enough for anyone. The life of a teenage girl is comprised of comparing. They compare themselves to everyone around them, all of the time! How can they measure up to the airbrushed supermodels, the teenage sex icons, the music video and movie "hotties?" Then, there are the girls in their classes, the "good" girls, the "bad" girls, and all the other versions of who they "should" be. The examples in many of their lives have said in so many words, "If you are not enough on your own, then fix it, buy it, or have surgery to correct it." Meanwhile, these wounded hearts are trying to answer the main questions that every teenager has to face in life: Who loves me, and why am I important?

Several years ago, I began to see how all this was taking hold in the lives of some of my teenage friends. While reading up on some studies to share with girls, I found several on the topic of humility. As I read through them, I thought, "Humility? Wow, sadly I don't think many of these girls even like themselves." Harsh, but it stopped me in my tracks. So many times and in so many ways, I had heard that negative thought spoken and lived out in the lives of my young friends. Teenage girls crave love—real love—and yet they have such a hard time receiving it and believing they are worth it. Many have no idea what it looks like to be loved well or to believe they are lovable. In recent years, I've noticed young women are struggling more with the primary questions, "Who loves me?" and "Why am I important?" than I have seen in the past. Many of them simply do not love themselves, and they certainly don't see themselves as important. So in their minds, why would anyone else see value in them?

I've also watched girls return from amazing camp experiences and fall prey to the world's demands and lies. The Lord's presence is the one place we should be able to come, be ourselves, and feel complete, whole, loved and enough. I realized that these young girls needed help seeing that! To go home from camp and live out that reality seemed an insurmountable obstacle for some. I asked myself:

How do you live as someone loved, if that is a new reality for you?

What if you've never had someone show you true, unconditional, father-like love?

What if you hate your body, your uniqueness, and yourself?

What if you don't believe you're worth loving because you just aren't _____ enough?

Sadly, these are real thoughts for so many girls today.

At the time, my daughter was about four years old. She was feisty, spunky, unique, constantly covered in dirt, food and she was undeniably beautiful and such a treasure! How I hoped, and still do, that no one could cause her to think otherwise. I wanted to be a positive voice in the ears of my daughter as well as other young women, to encourage them to embrace and believe the treasure they were created to be. By doing so, they would honor the Lord who put us together.

This desire led me to begin intentionally talking with teenage girls about how loved they are by their heavenly Father, how to love the God who made them, and how to find beauty in themselves. Still, I saw a need to discuss their unspoken hurts and frustrations even more, so I put together a seminar to do just that—to encourage young women to see themselves as treasures, unique, and valuable—to see themselves as God sees them, and to challenge them to see those things in others.

The simple seminar we put together is still evolving and changing, but just the chance to discuss some of these issues aloud had a tremendous impact on me and on many of the young women we have shared with. This same seminar has been presented primarily to girls in middle school, high school, college and some older adult settings. It has touched women from urban, rural and suburban areas and from all different socio-economic, racial, faith and geographical backgrounds. We received feedback that the seminar was "life-changing," "changed everything," "incredible" and that it "changed everything." Why was this so important to so many young women? The seminar itself wasn't perfect, and the content wasn't anything new, but the need must have been greater than even I realized. I learned that young women desperately wanted to know that they were not alone in their feelings and insecurities.

Here is how the hour unfolds for our time together. Before entering, every woman picks up a rock from outside. We begin with some dialogue and, in all honesty, the first time I led this I wasn't sure how it would go. But, without fail, women of all ages have been unbelievably honest and real as we ask questions and open up discussion around the subject of how they see themselves and the pressures they feel. Next, I pull out pictures and ads from all kinds of recent magazines and paste them on poster boards. I ask, "What do you see?" The girls fire back words like skinny, perfect, clear skin, tall, big boobs, long legs, great hair, rich, and successful. Then comes the next question: "How do these pictures make you feel?" The answers come a little more slowly this time, but usually after one brave girl starts with something honest, the others join in. The words are hard to hear, but every girl nods her head as they listen to others say the words that inevitably are always spoken: fat, ugly, imperfect, not enough, can't measure up, failure and on and on. I ask how many girls thought that they were the only one who felt like that and almost every single hand goes up. Immediately, a feeling of solidarity and disbelief spreads, as the girls look around at a room full of hands.

To underscore the fact that they are not alone, we list these statistics:

> More than 80% of 4th grade girls have been on a fad diet says "SIRC"—Social Issues Research Center.

> Dove Campaign for Real Beauty, Dove (a beauty product company) commissioned a global study to explore self-esteem and the impact of beauty ideals on both women's and girls' lives (2005) found that 90% of women ages 15-64 worldwide want to change at least one aspect of physical appearance, with body weight being the highest.

> Sixty-seven percent (2/3) of women withdraw from engaging in life activities, because they feel bad about themselves. More than half of us don't do things because we don't like who we are.

In other words, we aren't living fully because we are paralyzed by our thoughts. We are held captive by our insecurities. We believe that the outside is all that matters and that it has to be a certain way. We compare ourselves to the standard or ideal that the world has set, and when we don't fit that mold, we lose confidence, doubt ourselves and don't live out who we were created to be. Ultimately, our insecurity has become the silent killer of girls and even older women.

The Dove website has an amazing video (*Evolution*) that shows a model coming in for a photo-shoot. They take a picture and then photo-shop it to change her cheekbones, her nose, her eyebrows and almost every part of her into the "ideal" look. In the end, the billboard goes up, and the model looks nothing like she does in reality. "No wonder our perception of beauty is distorted," the video says. As I show that to the girls, their eyes widen and their jaws drop. What a shock! When I ask for their response, the girls inevitably want to watch it again, and they are always in awe that what they see around them isn't real. The standard that is held up to them, to which they aspire, feels like a lie. Girls are frustrated, mad, irritated, and relieved all at the same time. They "had no idea" that they had been comparing themselves and trying to live up to an ideal that was created, designed, and manipulated. They feel cheated by the media, and mad that the world around them seems so unfair and so fake. We have listened to the world around us and not to God, and we see ourselves as less than who God has made us to be.

As the seminar continues, we talk about the fact that when we listen to the world around us and not to God, it is easy to see ourselves as less than we are and less than what God made us to be—a masterpiece! I show a drawing of a girl that my daughter spent a lot of time creating. She painstakingly colored in the details, and when it was just right she declared that she was finished. A work of art! I ask, "What if the picture miraculously came to life?" What if this beauty, this masterpiece and work of art by my daughter, was miraculously living and breathing? Well, my daughter would be thrilled! She would be just how my daughter pictured, imagined, and dreamt she would be. But then, what if things changed? What if, to my daughter's surprise, the girl in the picture looked at herself and asked why her hair is blonde, why her lips are so big, why her eyes are the color they are, and continues with critique to her designer. I ask the girls how my daughter would feel, and they empathetically say how sad that would be. They all agree that it would break her heart. So, I say, if you are a work of God's design and His masterpiece, how do you think He feels when you tear yourself apart?

From there, we look at two Bible passages: Ephesians 2:10 ("For we are God's masterpiece, created in Christ Jesus to do good works, which God prepared in advance for us to do") and Psalm 139:13-38, which talks about being carefully and wonderfully made. We don't often understand how amazing it is that the God of the universe spent time on us, and that He spent a lot of energy and love on us. We are no accident, and we are wonderfully made. What a concept! This is a starting point. Many girls have never thought of themselves as a masterpiece, as a work of beauty, or even as valuable at all. Many do not have people in their lives who affirm their worth and beauty. Many do not understand the unconditional father-like love of God, because they have never seen it in their own lives. Their value has been in their accomplishments, their performance, or the superficial.

Sadly, many girls begin to look in negative directions for the affirmation, love, and attention that they so desperately crave. When we ask, "The world can be hard, can't it?" teenagers breathe a sigh of relief that someone gets it. And, when we ask, "What do you as a teenage girl feel the pressure to be like?" we get an earful in return. Girls join together and finish the sentence "I feel like I need to be . . ." The physical descriptions come first. "I feel like I need to be . . . pretty, skinny, have perfect skin, tall, good hair."

Then they start to think deeper, and they finish the sentence with words like, ". . . good student, smart (but not too smart, some girls say), popular, sexy, athletic, feminine, good, bad."

That's a lot of pressure! These are many of the same struggles women of all ages face. In today's culture, however, these pressures are increased exponentially by the media and these young girls often don't have the tools or positive relationships in their lives to help them combat the onslaught. I ask the girls in the seminar to think about the following statements: "We are in an abusive relationship with ourselves. We beat ourselves up and say things to ourselves we would never let anyone else say." I ask the girls if they agree, and they look at one another, nod their heads in unison, and laugh, "Yeah, why do we do that?"

If we can stop obsessing and dwelling on ourselves, we can then move on to bless others around us. If girls can get past their own hang-ups and pitfalls, they can actually begin to move out into the world in ways they have never done before, and this generation can be a mighty force. When we embrace who we are, we can move forward and more fully embrace others. That's when great stuff happens!

We need help remembering the truth, because it is so much easier to believe lies. In the seminar, I give a few examples from my own life about negative comments that stuck with me. I cannot for the life of me remember anything positive that anyone said. I grew up in a great family and had great friends, but nothing specific sticks in my memory. However, I vividly recall two instances growing up where I was teased, and those particular words stuck with me. Why do the negative things stick in our minds, and the positive things do not? It just shows how important it is to help one another out, and to realize the power of our words.

So many young girls have a long list of words they have heard about themselves and those words replay over and over in their minds until they start to believe they are true. We need to stop listening to what the world around us (MTV, TV, movies, music videos and magazines) tells us to be like and listen instead to who God says that we are. God says what is true. We talk about the fact that it isn't easy, and that we need to remind ourselves every day of the truth and cover up the lies. To reinforce that idea, we take the three poster boards with the magazine pictures—our current measuring stick for worth and beauty—and we cover them with scripture—with what God says. The verses we use are:

> **Psalm 45:11**—Let the king be enthralled by your beauty; honor him, for he is your lord.

> **Zephaniah 3:17**—The Lord your God is with you, the Mighty Warrior who saves. He will take great delight in you; in his love he will no longer rebuke you, but will rejoice over you with singing.

> **Psalm 139:13-18**—For you created my inmost being; you knit me together in my mother's womb. I praise you because I am fearfully and wonderfully made; your works are wonderful, I know that full well.

My friend, Carly Calmes, was part of the "program team" at camp and had been up front on stage all week. Carly also has a passion for young women and a heart to share her own journey as an encouragement for others, so I asked her to join us. She was so excited that she wrote a song about being a masterpiece and we have been blessed many times to have her share it as part of our time together. Carly is a talented singer-songwriter and has joined me several times at summer camp as she leads our music. Before she sings, she talks about her own struggles in embracing who God has made her to be. Carly beautifully tells of her adolescence and her insecurities about her looks and her personality. She describes being at camp and not going outside during free time because she didn't want to get in a swimsuit. She also recalls a feeling of being "too much" and trying not to be—too loud, too silly, too "much." Carly talks about understanding who she is as a child of God, as someone of His design, and ultimately as a masterpiece. She talks about discovering her uniqueness as a gift, and because of that she then gained the confidence to begin to sing.

Carly is an amazingly gifted person on stage. She has led kids in games and dances and her silliness and humor have been a gift to thousands of teenagers who have enjoyed her and laughed with her. She has allowed others to see that it is okay to be silly, to have fun and to be yourself. In addition, Carly is an amazing singer and she has a voice of an angel. The girls at camp have seen Carly upfront and onstage all week. They have seen her as beautiful, talented and unafraid. And then, they hear her story and realize that her gifts were not always understood and embraced. Even Carly struggles with the same things they do. Carly then shares an amazing song with the girls, including this chorus:

And I know that you don't think it's true
That I see so much beauty in you
But I'll fight for you darling, believe
That there's no one who loves you like me
You're mine
You're my masterpiece
You're mine
You're a part of me
You're mine
I made your heart, it's my fine art

We remind girls that they are created beautifully by Him—that they are valuable because He says so! The God of the universe says so! No matter what they may feel about themselves, or even what others may have told them, God says they're amazing and valuable, loved, accepted and wanted.

As we continue, I use an analogy I heard long ago about a dollar bill. While holding up a dollar bill, we have this brief exchange:

Me: How much is this bill worth?
Girls: One dollar!
Me: Who assigns this dollar bill its value?
Girls: The U.S. Government/Treasury
Me: Why? Because they made it, and the maker determines the value.

Then I explain, No matter what you do to the dollar bill—you can wad it up, step on it, fold it up, or even spit on it—it is still worth a dollar, because the maker says so. We can be mistreated (and many young women have been), treated unkindly, disrespected, felt like we have been stepped on, wadded up, or even thrown away, but our value never changes in the eyes of our Maker. We are valuable, not because of what we look like, what we do, or what others may say. We are valuable because God has declared us so! We get so desperate to feel worth something and feel valuable and loved that we look to the wrong places (clothes, sports, stuff, accomplishments, boys). So often, we girls get in trouble because we don't respect ourselves and we really don't believe that we are valuable, so we go chasing for that sense of value in the wrong places. But God has created us, inside and out, with talents, spiritual gifts, things we are good at and enjoy, personalities that are different, goals, ways of thinking and interests. There is a special job for each of us in this world.

God had a special job for a young girl named Amy Carmichael. Long ago, Amy was a missionary to India. As a young girl, Amy wanted blue eyes instead of her brown eyes. She prayed for blue eyes, and her prayers went seemingly unanswered. However, God used Amy's brown eyes for a purpose. Years later, in India, Amy was able to blend in while covered—with only her brown eyes showing. Because of this, she was able to help young teenage girls escape from forced prostitution. If Amy had blue eyes, she wouldn't have blended in or been able to rescue the girls. Amy was brave, compassionate, bold and she had brown eyes. God has purposes for how He made us—inside and out.

What an amazing thing it would be if we could love and embrace who we are and who we are not. I will never be a singer like Carly and I will never be tall, have curly hair, or many other things. I do know, however, that I can step into what He has put before me and live in that. How different if we believed this and treated others as if they, too, were treasures of the Lord! What if we looked for ways to use the way God has made us and to help others do the same? We are valuable because of Him—because we bear the stamp of the Creator and not because of anything else! He has declared our value, and we can be set free from feelings of worthlessness! What is truly beautiful is His reflection in us!

What if we lived like this? Let's be real. How different would life be if we believed this and treated others as if they, too, were treasures and masterpieces? What if we looked for ways to use the way God has made us, and we helped others to do the same instead of comparing ourselves to one another all the time? Galatians 5:26 in *The Message* says, ". . . we will not compare ourselves with each other as if one of us were better and another worse. We have far more important things to do with our lives. Each of us is an original."

We have wrapped up our seminar with a few things that have been incredibly powerful in ways I could have never foreseen. One way is that the girls come to the front and symbolically exchange the rock they brought with them for a new one. "We carry around an inadequate view of ourselves as average, not special, lumpy, plain, like the rocks you brought in," I tell them. We ask girls to exchange that for a new "rock," and a new idea of who they are. There are piles of gems of different colors, sizes, and shapes, and the girls pick out a new gem and leave the old rock behind. We tell them to put their gem someplace where they will see it regularly, to serve as a visual reminder to them.

I can't tell you how many girls I have seen years later, who tell me that they still have their gem in their purse, their car, their backpack or their nightstand. They say it really helps remind them of their true value, on days that their worth feels threatened. Wow!

A second powerful conclusion to the seminar has been small groups. We let the girls sit in small groups with their friends and answer one question together. We ask them to discuss, "If you really believed this and lived as if it were true, how would your life be different?" It is unbelievable to hear their answers. They would do more, love more and live more. They would be kinder to others, more compassionate and more themselves. By shedding their own stuff, they could help others see their beauty. It is unbelievably encouraging to hear young girls want to step beyond their paralysis, and have vision beyond their walls.

Although girls were responding well to this seminar, and we had positive feedback, something was missing. I didn't even see it. In 2011, Alan Smyth approached me as we finished a week of the seminar and asked if he could say something from the perspective of a father. Alan and I had been friends for several years and I knew his big heart for his daughter and other teenage girls. I believed that he would say something that assuredly would be great for them to hear. I'm not sure why I had never thought of including that perspective before, because of course there is significant value in hearing from a male/father perspective!

Alan's contribution to the seminar added great value. He proved to be an integral part, and I will never again do this seminar without a voice of a father saying things that every young girl should grow up hearing: "You are valuable, you are a princess, you are important and so very amazing and beautiful." Alan echoed the heart of God for them as he talked of his love for his daughter, his desire to protect her and his heart to see the best for her and in her. I looked around the room as girls' eyes were focused on Alan, many brimming with tears. I saw them sit up straighter and smile as he told them they should act as princesses because that is what they are. I watched them soak up every word from this man they did not know well, but who was there to let them in on a vision of a good father. A father that he admitted may not exist for each of them. Many girls in that room had never heard much at all positive from a male, whether a young man their age or an adult.

Many young girls have an incredibly difficult time understanding and accepting God's love when they have not seen that kind of unconditional fatherly love in action in their lives. How hard it is to understand, believe, and accept what you have no vision of in your life.

Unfortunately, although girls so crave positive attention from men and especially their fathers, they so rarely get it. I have seen it in the lives of the girls I have worked with over the years. I have seen them soak in any attention they can get.

I have also watched as my own husband has been the affirming, positive voice in the lives of many teenage girls in the absence of their fathers. I watched a young girl who did not grow up with a father figure and was afraid of heights finish a challenge course at camp. As I hugged her when she got down, she said, "I can't wait to go find Coach Fox and tell him! He'll be so proud of me!" (She was referring to my husband.) As I hid the tears welling up in my eyes, I understood that in that moment and so many others in her life, she had craved a father figure to encourage her, to applaud her courage, and to simply say, "Well done."

She and so many other young girls have missed that most of their lives. Some of them have absent fathers, some have neglectful fathers, and some just have busy and distracted fathers.

I think we often underestimate the voice and presence of a father or a positive male figure in the lives of young girls. The words of a father should echo the voice of God. It is not an easy world, girls hear too much garbage, and they need a father's voice saying, "You are enough as you are, I love you, you are valuable, and you can trust me."

Alan conveyed that sentiment to these girls week after week. They heard from him what they should have been hearing for the past 15 years, and many had not. Life-changing? Yes. For some young girls who have not heard that growing up, I've heard their hearts say, "If my dad doesn't love me for who I am, then what guy will?"

We need men to stand before their daughters and say those words they crave and long to hear, so that they do not go searching for it elsewhere. It is that voice that can help demonstrate the passion, compassion, heart, unconditional love, encouragement, and even correction of the heavenly Father. Men, please be a conduit of the voice of God to the girls and women around you. God is whispering in the ears of these young girls, and fathers need to repeat the heart of God, loud and clear.

Real Talk

"In my 16 years of leading Young Life, I can tie nearly every single girl's self-confidence to her relationship with her dad. Everyone wants approval, but the approval of a father for his daughter is beyond impactful. I have had girls verbalize that they are having sex with their boyfriends to get their dads' attention, to prove to their dad that they are worthy of being loved, to show their dad someone wants them, or to make their dad feel like what he thinks of her doesn't matter."

Chapter 5

Alan's Part of the Seminar

"One girl described the girl talk with Alan as the most impactful part of camp. She has two absent fathers and said she really needed to hear what was said."

"The talk from Alan at the girls' time was LIFE-CHANGING for a few of my girls. Thank you!"

"The talk you gave was a HUGE deal for my girls. They haven't had a protective father to ever tell them they are a princess."

The above statements are direct quotes that I heard last summer, after I spoke for just ten minutes to a room of high school girls at Young Life camp. It is common practice that during the last few days of Young Life camp, the staff offers various seminars for the campers. By now, the wild and crazy fun that Young Life camps are known for has wound down, and the tenor of camp has shifted to a more thoughtful and contemplative mood. Deeper issues are discussed, and the content goes to a much deeper level. The camp schedule also opens up by the end of the week, providing more free time to facilitate high quality conversations between campers and their leaders.

Often, one of these seminars we offer may be on the topic of guy/girl relationships, family issues, sex and dating, body image and more. The exact seminar depends on which camp staff is present, and their area of expertise. During this particular camp assignment, Kristy Fox served as one of the head leaders. Kristy is a veteran Regional Director in Young Life, and has served in Southern California since the early 90's. I met Kristy in 1993 at a Young Life camp when she brought a car full of girls to a week where I was the camp speaker. Since then, we've had several camp assignments together, seen each other at numerous Young Life staff events, and become good friends.

I was excited to learn that Kristy would be on my assignment team last summer for several reasons. First, she is a friend and a great teammate. Secondly, Kristy is very experienced and skilled at all the jobs at Young Life camp. I was also excited she would be there because I knew that she has often led a seminar specifically targeting the girls in camp. I had seen her do this before, and witnessed its impact. Kristy has crafted an hour-long, interactive seminar for girls that includes several illustrations. It is full of Bible verses, videos, and activities designed to change the way young girls view themselves, and teach what God thinks about them. I was certain that I could get Kristy to lead her seminar again for our camp weeks.

I have a big heart for the topic of young girls gaining self-confidence, a proper perspective and healing. During our first week of camp, I snuck in the back of the girls' only seminar so I could listen in. I wanted to see what I could learn and I also wanted to simply enjoy the conversation. The seminar progressed and it was incredible. Kristy does a great job communicating to young girls what God thinks about them and therefore what they should think of themselves. It was creative, informative, and engaging. She had great stories, great Scripture and a great video. However, as I listened, I thought that perhaps an important item was being left out. Everything Kristy did was amazing, but as a guy, I thought something was missing.

So, reluctantly, I approached Kristy after her seminar and said as much. I told her that, while I thought everything was great, maybe there was room for another perspective as well. I told her that I thought it was important for young girls to hear a dad's viewpoint. I knew that hearing something positive from a strong male is something that is missing in the lives of many, if not most, young girls. Also, I thought that we might be missing an opportunity with a room full of girls if we didn't talk straight with them about the minds of young males. Obviously Kristy would not be able to speak to that issue, so I offered my services. Not wanting to barge in on her seminar, I told her that if she thought there was any value in adding a few minutes from a dad's and guy's perspective, that I would be happy to do so. Kristy thanked me, and we went on our way. I didn't bring it up again for the rest of the week, because it wasn't something I was pushing for, and what she was doing was already great.

We did not talk about it again over the entire next week. Still, I knew that in order for these girls to view God correctly, that they had to have a better picture of an earthly father. Since I also knew that so many of them were lacking in that regard, I wanted to stand in and attempt to paint a picture they could grasp. Nancy Pantellas, then a 25-year Young Life veteran, said this:

> Having been in many summer camp cabin times and
> many Bible studies, the greatest heartache I have seen, and

the most tears that have been cried, is over the absence of a dad. So many of the troubles in those teen years (and adult, too) can be traced back to that absentee father. Two of the most important roles of the father are (1) to model to their daughters what a gentleman is and how their daughters should expect to be treated by men, (2) to model how precious, protected, accepted and beloved they girls are in their Heavenly Father's eyes.

My friend Jaimee adds,

A broken relationship with her earthly father will rob or withhold the riches and sweetness of the treasures God has intended for His daughter. Stripping her of the most precious part of her identity in Christ, it will force her to fill that void with all manner of empty pursuits and dangerous ideas. She will find herself battling the spirits of fear, abandonment, loneliness, helplessness, and self-loathing. No one and nothing can replace the unique love of a father or his precious place in her life.

We had a tall task in front of us. The stakes were high with the girls in the room. Seven days went by. During our second week of camp on the morning of Kristy's seminar, I was driving in a golf cart down the back road of the property, when I heard Kristy's voice calling for me over the radio. She laughed apologetically, and asked if I was still willing to share in her seminar. She said that she was sorry for the late notice, and had intended to ask earlier, but had gotten busy and forgot.

I said, "Sure, I would be happy to share. When is it?"

Kristy laughed. "It starts in five minutes."

I chuckled and replied, "Well, I don't need a lot of prep time to talk about father/daughter relationships and what I think about young girls, and more importantly, what God thinks about them." I said I would come right up.

Kristy's seminar had begun by the time I walked in the back of the room. About 15 minutes into her talk, she introduced me. I walked to the front, and, in a rather impromptu and spur of the moment fashion, I shared the following thoughts. As unprepared and unpolished as they seemed to me, apparently my thoughts were significant to the room of high schools girls.

I began by sharing my perspective on my daughter Brittany. I shared with these girls the little game I had created with Brittany about calling her my "Prized Possession." I walked them through our call and response:

"What are you?"

"Your prized possession."

"And?"

"Don't you forget it!"

There were probably 175 high school girls in that room, and you could have heard a pin drop. I don't think they knew that kind of relationship could exist between fathers and daughters. Sadly, so many girls feel anything but valued by anyone, let alone their own dads. And, sadly, most young girls feel their dads have more important things to do in their life. I think the healing process was beginning for some girls in the first few minutes of my sharing.

Next, I talked about them as royalty. Earlier in the spring, a royal wedding had taken place. The images and hype about Princess Kate and Prince William's London wedding were fresh in everyone's mind. Everyone was talking about the celebration, uniqueness and elevated status of Princess Kate, and her beauty and class were obvious. It was obvious, too, that millions of people respected and admired her. I told the girls that God views them as His precious daughter. "If He is King of the universe," I asked, "and you are His daughter, then what does that make you? What is the daughter of a king called?"

Several of the girls blurted, "A princess!"

I said, "Yes, you are a princess. Did anyone ever call you a princess before?"

One girl yelled, "YES! Finally!" The room burst out into laughs and cheers.

Hearing that God viewed them as princesses and that they should be treated as such, seemed to strike a chord with so many of them. Who in the world is treating these girls like royalty? Who refers to them as a princess? Who respects and admires them? Sadly, they hear many words and phrases used to describe them through the media, music, TV, movies and the males around them that I'm sure break God's heart and no doubt do significant damage to their souls. What girls can take away from popular song lyrics, locker room talk and general communication from society is anything but respectful, adoring and admiring. They are generally referred to as anything but princesses. What a breath of fresh air for a battered 16-year-old girl to hear that someone thinks of her as a princess and that she should be treated as royalty. This short conversation seemed to have a big impact on many of the girls in the room. It is a massive paradigm shift for the vast majority of girls, both inside that room and out. How many problems could be avoided if somehow young girls could view themselves as God views them, and then live as though they believed it? What a gift we can give our girls!

Next, I shared with the crowd what I believe my role as a dad is. I said that I see myself as a defender and protector of Brittany. It started at birth, when the doctor placed my newborn little girl into my arms and said, "Here you go!" At that moment, the heart of a father instantly becomes that of a warrior on behalf of his little girl. The tuned-in father begins to embrace the idea of defending and protecting his sweet little girl. As his little girl grows, so does this concept in the mind and heart of her daddy.

Dads also begin to envision the day when boys start hovering. With fear and trepidation, a dad thinks about the day when his daughter explores the idea of a boyfriend. He's scared by this because, after all, he is a boy himself! He remembers what his thoughts and intentions were when he was a teenager. Now he imagines a pack of young males, similar to him and his friends, descending on his own little girl. Most young guys showing interest in a girl are clearly starting in a deficit position with her dad. They are in a deficit position before they have done anything at all . . . other than be a guy.

Most dads are extremely suspicious of any guy who starts hanging around. And for good reason I might add. Yet, I see a lot of dads who don't necessarily live with a healthy concern about boys hanging around their daughters. I would submit that this would be true for two reasons: Either, they have already disengaged from active parenting and in many ways have given up, or they simply don't have an accurate understanding of the environment their little girl is growing up in. They care, but they just don't know what I know.

I then told a brief version of when a certain young man started showing interest in my Brittany. This guy was good-looking, athletic, and charming. He was smooth and outgoing. He was extremely confident and sure of himself and was a couple of years older than Brittany. He was extremely attractive to Brittany, but he was extremely dangerous to me. I saw right through his game. He was a first-class "ladies' man," and he reminded me of some of my friends from high school. He also reminded me of many of the guys I had known over the years as a Young Life leader. The last thing in the world I wanted for my daughter was for a guy like him to see my daughter as another conquest.

I had two choices. I could either abdicate my role as defender and protector of my daughter and let things play out, or I could engage.

I'm guessing you know which one I chose. I did a little research, asking around to people who knew him. I was friends with one of the teachers from his school, so I asked my friend what he thought about this guy. I heard things like, "always has a girlfriend," "seems like a player," and "seems like bad news." Translation to me . . . GAME ON.

All at once, I saw several things that really bothered me. First, he didn't have a car, so Brittany had to drive him everywhere. That bugged me. It drove me crazy that she would stay late at his house on a weekend night watching TV, and then have to drive herself home late. My mind envisioned her getting a flat tire or some other car trouble, and being out late, trying to fix it on her own. That bugged me. Then, the guy started getting overly comfortable in our home. He called me "Bro." I remember one instance when I came home to find him cooking himself hot dogs over my stove, and he greeted me with, "What's up Bro!?" That was about all I could take.

I saw my sweet little girl getting sucked in by his charm, and I saw him working his game. I knew what this looked like. I had seen it before. I am a guy! And I have been a Young Life leader to guys for some 30 years. I know well what they talk about and what they think about. I knew this was going to end badly if I didn't step in.

So, I had a little conversation with the young man. He was over at our house one night, watching TV. I knew that Brittany would have to drive him home late because, of course, he didn't have a car. I was sitting downstairs with them and I said, "Hey, how about I drive you home tonight?"

Brittany glared at me. She said, "I can take him home later."

I said, "No, that's okay! I'd be happy to take him home now. Don't worry about it." They looked awkwardly at each other, and with a slight eye roll, he got up and followed me out to my car. We made a little small talk as we drove, until I asked, "What are your intentions with my daughter?" He talked about how much he liked her, and said he wanted to pursue a relationship with her. I could see this was going to take awhile, so we pulled over into a dark parking lot and continued our conversation.

I knew he was lacking male input in his life and needed a little guidance and direction, so I shared with him the "path" of what it would take for him to spend more time with my daughter. I told him that he needed to start driving, get a job, and that he needed to meet with me regularly to discuss the Christian faith. I told him that I saw Brittany as my Prized Possession, and that I thought of her as a princess. I told him that Brittany was more valuable than anything that I had. I told him that I feared her getting a flat tire late at night, coming home from his house and struggling trying to fix it. I said, "Now, we have the princess out stranded late at night, trying to fix her own tire." I told him that, as a man, he needed to be willing to come and pick her up and drop her back off again. Not all of the time, I said, but at least some of the time. I let him know that it also bugged me that he didn't ever seem to have any money, so Brittany had to buy stuff for him all the time. I said that he needed to figure out a way to earn enough money to take her out and treat her once in a while. Most of all, I said, it concerned me that we did not share a common faith, and therefore he could not possibly have the same values that we had.

I never said that he couldn't spend time with Brittany. I simply gave him the path in which to do so. I thought I was giving him a gift of clarity! Then, I shifted the conversation to the potential physical side of their relationship. I let him know that we had raised Brittany with a certain set of values and expectations, and that I expected him to honor those values and expectations. I told him that, while in a parked car, in a dark parking lot, late at night, if he was to somehow cross that line—I gazed into the dark with a long, pregnant pause—that I "wasn't sure what I'd do." Then, I shook his hand, said I hoped we were clear on my expectations and his path to spending more time with my daughter, drove him home, and thanked him for the conversation. I shook his hand again and said good night.

Once more, as I relayed this tale to the girls in Kristy's seminar, you could have heard a pin drop. Oddly enough, they seemed to love this story. I'm guessing that none of them had ever had someone advocate for them like that before. Sadly, the idea of a dad defending and protecting their honor was a foreign concept for most of these girls. Most of them did not have a dad who would engage their boyfriends and let them know what the expectations were—if there were any at all. They needed to hear so badly that there was a dad out there willing to love and protect them. I acknowledged that many of them probably did not have a dad who was ready, willing, and able to rise to their defense. But, I said, "That is not your fault, and God Himself very much wants to be your heavenly Father, surrounding you with love and protection."

After I dropped the young man off at his house, he promptly got on the phone to Brittany and retold our conversation. Only, he told her that I said he could not spend time with her anymore. WRONG. That is not what I said. I simply gave him the conditions upon which he could do so. He then said his version of my expectations on their potential physical relationship. He told Brittany, "Your dad said that if I touched you, he'd kill me!"

Brittany responded, "Well, I'm sure he didn't mean that . . ."

But the boy interrupted her. "No, he did! And he could, too."

When Brittany relayed his words to me, I said, "Perfect! Then it looks like we have an understanding. Mission accomplished!"

I have never seen Brittany as mad as she was at that moment, and in the days to come. Looking back, I think it may be the only time in her life that she was actually mad at me, or at least seriously mad. She was furious that I would step in and put an end to this relationship. I kept remembering the Gunderson girls, and how they said, "Even if she pushes you away, don't give up!"

After a few days, when she had cooled off a bit, Brittany came into my bedroom one night as Sharon and I watched TV. During our conversation, I reiterated that this guy was bad news, and that spending time with him was a mistake. She asked me why I couldn't just let her make her own mistakes.

"Think about what you are asking me to do," I said. "You are asking me to sit on the bank of a river, and wave at you as you float by on a raft, when all the while I know that just around the river bend is Niagara Falls! You are asking me to smile at you and watch you go over the falls for the sake of letting you make your own mistakes." I told her that was something I was simply not willing to do, and that it was my job as her dad to defend and protect her whenever possible. In the end, I said, I was willing to have her mad at me now and then if it meant keeping her safe.

My primary goal was not to have her happy with me. My primary goal was her safety. I also reminded her that I did not tell this guy he couldn't see her again. I simply said that he needed to begin treating her like a princess. I asked Brittany if she wanted to be treated like a princess. "Doesn't that sound pretty good?" I asked. "Don't you think you deserve to be treated like a princess?" I told her, too, that we would soon see what kind of guy he was, and what his true intentions were. If he got his act together and began working on my conditions, then we would know that he might be a good guy worthy of spending time with and actually interested in a relationship. However, if my suspicions were correct, we might never see him again, and we would know for sure what his real intentions were.

I'll let you guess what happened.

I actually think this seminar full of girls at Young Life camp was longing to hear something like this. Even though it did not happen to them, it restored some hope that there were dads out there, willing to step into the lives of their daughters and provide guidance and protection. I think it was somehow healing for them to hear this story, as some of them were living vicariously through this situation. The norm is an absentee father who is either gone in spirit or gone in body. I think it encouraged them to hear how it was supposed to be, and to know that somebody wanted to protect them.

The final few minutes of my part of Kristy's seminar dealt with an inside look at a typical male. I told them that I was going to give them a gift and speak candidly about what was happening inside the brain of an average guy. I told them that I was perfectly qualified to speak on this because I had been a guy pretty much my whole life and was an expert on the topic. The girls chuckled, and I continued.

I pointed out some of the basic differences between men and women—that most guys are extremely physical and visual in their thinking and processing, much more than the average girl. I let the girls know that most young guys were thinking sexual thoughts almost all the time. Not literally all the time, but pretty darn close. I explained that guys are primarily driven physically, while most girls are primarily driven emotionally. It wasn't that guys didn't want to connect with them at the deepest possible place, but it was more that they couldn't. I told them that we simply were not wired like they were, and that we are incapable of understanding their deep emotions and moods.

Then I began to see them as a room full of daughters, and I wanted to protect them and warn them. I let them know that, while there were certainly lots of great guys out there, that there were also lots of predators and scumbags. I told them that there were a lot of guys out there who didn't care about them at all, but rather only saw them as a "thing." I told them that some of these guys would tell them they loved them, if that meant that would get them into bed.

I shared with the girls that there were plenty of guys out there with good intentions, but that even for the best guy out there, it was a huge struggle for him to do the right thing and treat a girl the way she deserved to be treated. As a guy goes through his day prewired to be highly sensitive to things that are visual and physical, he is inundated with thousands upon thousands of images that degrade women and promote unhealthy behavior. It's no wonder that so many young guys are so preoccupied with sex and selfishness. The world loudly preaches a promiscuous lifestyle. Even more, the world celebrates, glamorizes and rewards it.

Furthermore, since many dads are absent in a meaningful way to young boys as well, they lack proper guidance and accountability. I let these girls know that they could really help guys out with their clothing choices. "Showing a lot of skin and cleavage will be advertising something that might not be for sale," I told them. "It will be communicating something to a guy that you might not be intending to communicate." I acknowledged that it's tough to buy cute, modest clothing and swimwear, but I said that they needed to know that dressing in a revealing way is like throwing gas on a fire in the mind of a young male (or any age). As I began to talk about just how often a young male is said to have a sexual thought, jaws began to drop. Most of these girls seemed completely stunned by this conversation. It was as if they had just discovered the world was round.

I suppose that no trusted male figure had ever let them know what a guy is actually thinking. I am guessing that most of these girls had never had anyone ever tell them what their clothing choice is shouting to the guys around them, nor had they been given any guidelines in that regard. I then closed with a few remarks, reminding them that they are God's masterpiece and a daughter of the God of the universe. I reminded them that they are princesses and that they should expect to be treated as such. I urged them to not lower their standards for some guy who didn't really care about them anyway. I urged them to keep the bar high and hold out for a guy who was willing to treat them like a princess and respect them enough to wait until they got married. I told them that any guy not willing to respect them and treat them like a princess was not worth their time and worthy of their heart.

Again, you could have heard a pin drop as most of these girls had never been challenged to keep the bar high. They had never been told that they were worth the very best and shouldn't settle for anything less. No one is speaking these ideas into the hearts of our young girls. Not the world, media, music, movies, or TV. And very sadly, not many of our dads.

Natalie, one of our female Young Life leaders who works in a very urban environment in Los Angeles, said this to me after the seminar:

> Many of my girls seek their worth in what a boy thinks
> of them. This is why the talk you gave was a HUGE deal
> for my girls. They haven't had a protective father to ever
> tell them they are princesses and to wait for the man who

treats them as one. Never had the experience of being embarrassed by their dad who grills a boy when they are picked up for a date. In fact, the girls aren't usually asked on dates. They don't know what it's like to have a man cherish them from the moment they were born or to have their father be the first man to ever tell them how beautiful and perfect they are. These girls are desperate for the love and appreciation of a male and usually accept it from the first boy at school who says they will give that to them.

After I said all this in about ten minutes, I sat down and enjoyed the rest of Kristy's seminar. I wish the words I had spoken in this seminar didn't seem that impactful. They seemed basic and simplistic to me, yet deep, profound, and healing to so many girls. The fact that they seemed so powerful is a measuring stick, showing where so many father/daughter relationships are today. It also speaks to the state of our young girls and further heightens the need for intense focus in this area.

Real Talk

"Most of the promiscuity I've seen in my girls can be attributed to a lack of a father figure pouring into her. I have a girl who has a great, Godly dad who loves her, but he's so wrapped up in his boys and their sports and his work that she doesn't feel invested in. She resents him. She has turned to a way of life she doesn't even want. I have several girls who don't believe in long-term relationships because their parents aren't together anymore. They think leaving someone is how life is meant to be. Even those girls who have dads that are good to them are greatly affected by how the dad treats the mom."

Chapter 6

Engaging: From Dads, for Dads

Field-tested, practical ideas from dads

In a critical, climactic scene in the movie *Top Gun*, Tom Cruise, a.k.a. Maverick, and his cohorts flying F-16's battle the dreaded "MIGS." Maverick had been traumatized earlier when his good friend, Goose, was killed in a training exercise. By now, Maverick was flying again, though he still struggled to enter into the fight. As he continued to circle outside of the battle, Maverick was distracted and preoccupied. He was near the battle, but not IN the battle. His commander back on the ship screamed, "Engage, Maverick! Engage!" Soon, Maverick did engage, and he eventually won the battle.

That scene reminds me of a lot of dads out there, who are circling the battle yet staying out of it. If that is you, I want to scream, "ENGAGE!" The battle you're avoiding is swirling around your daughter, and she needs you to engage. You are distracted and preoccupied with your own world, not realizing there is a battle raging around your daughter. In this chapter, we'll hear the stories of dads who have engaged and done it well. It's your chance to learn from some "Top Gun" dads.

I concluded Chapter 2 with my strong resolution about how I was going to move forward in my parenting of Brittany. Certainly my resolution at that time did not cover the totality of my developing parenting strategy, but it was definitely a strong feeling impressed upon me at that time. The "Grand Slam of Input," which came from four distinct conversations, led to one very strong resolution that caused me to think creatively about spending time with my daughter from then on.

> **My Resolution: I will do everything within my power to give Brittany all the resources, love, affection and attention she needs to make good and life-giving choices in her life. Should Brittany end up making some poor choices later in her life, it will not be because her dad wasn't involved with her or didn't love her well.**

I resolved that Brittany needed a strong, positive male figure in her life. She needed her dad to be engaged and spend constant and consistent time with her for the next 15 years. This is in no way meant to diminish the role of her mother. Sharon has been a spectacular mom to both of our kids. As a mom, Sharon provided the nurturing, guidance, and encouragement that only a mother can give. But I believe that God created a perfect model for parenting. He intended that there would be both a mom and a dad to speak differently into the lives of children. Sharon did her job superbly! I tried to do my job, as well. Through my Grand Slam of Input and my subsequent resolution, I came up with a few gems that I incorporated over the next 15 years. I'll share them with you here, and then follow them up with a number of other dads who have raised their daughters well. Let's learn from those who have gone before us!

Father/Daughter Getaway

The first, strongest, and by far most celebrated strategy I stumbled upon was the "Father/Daughter Getaway." In my desire to spend quality and significant time with Brittany, I suggested we start a new tradition. The summer just before she started Kindergarten, I suggested the soon-to-become famous "Father/Daughter Getaway," I remember tucking her into bed one night, and bringing up my plans to her.

"At the end of the summer, before school starts," I asked, "I think we should have the first ever Father/Daughter Getaway!"

"What is that?" she asked.

I explained that we were going to begin a new tradition, and that every summer, the two of us would plan a fun trip together. At that time, we lived in Northern California, and she was five years old. I wanted to start off with a bang, so naturally the best thing I could suggest was . . . Disneyland! She had been a couple times before, so she was very excited, as any five-year-old would be. As the time approached, I dubbed a mix cassette tape (yes, cassette tape!) entitled "FDG Soundtrack." I took all of the recent Disney movie soundtracks, and recorded the hit songs, one after the other. We drove all the way to Los Angeles rocking out to "I Just Can't Wait to be King," "I Can Show You the World," "Hakuna Matata," "Be Our Guest," and more. We must have played that tape four or five times from start to finish on our road trip down, just getting pumped for our adventure together.

Alan & Brittany Smyth on their first
Father/Daughter get away

Brittany and I got a hotel room, early admission to the park, pictures with all the characters, and the obligatory picture in front with the flowers and train station behind us. And of course, we rode lots of rides. We ran around from one end of the park to the other in a completely inefficient manner. It would have made much more sense to finish one "land" at a time before moving to the land next door. But who was there to make sense? Who was there to be efficient? I was there with a five-year-old little girl who was spending unprecedented amounts of time with her daddy. When she had the idea to go on the next ride, which happened to be clear across the park, I said, "Let's go!" We ate frozen bananas, popcorn, burgers, and all kinds of treats. We disregarded normal bedtimes and watched fireworks late into the evening. We did whatever we wanted to do, and had not a care in the world. The days were long and the fun was huge! She held my hand as we walked through crowds, because my guard was always up.

What a phenomenal time we had, just the two of us in Disneyland. Even better was the nonverbal tradition that was started on that trip. On that trip, we began a rich tradition between the two of us. Each year, we'd start planning what she wanted to do for our next Father/Daughter Getaway. I never really said it out loud, but Brittany began to understand that her dad wanted to spend time with her. She began to internalize that she and her daddy were going on trips together, and that her dad had fun with her. She also began to understand that her dad was not afraid to spend a little money on the things we did. Rather than pinch pennies and communicate one thing, we went big and had fun, in hopes of communicating how very "worth it" she was.

Alan & Brittany on another So Cal Father/Daughter get away in Jr. High

As Brittany grew older so did the Father/Daughter Getaways. One year it was camping in a tent, a bonfire, and s'mores. Another year featured horseback riding, because that is what she was excited about. As she entered junior high, we made another SoCal road trip because she became interested in the Hollywood scene. We drove up as high as we could to take a picture of the Hollywood sign. We ate at the Hard Rock Café, and walked up and down Hollywood Blvd. Another year we determined to hit every major shopping mall in the Bay Area, and take a picture in front of the marquees. While we were at it, we did all of our family Christmas shopping that August!

But the highlight "FDG," as we began to call it, was during her senior year of high school. That year, Brittany approached me and said, "You know, Dad, since this is our last Father/Daughter Getaway, we need to do something big!"

"First of all," I said, "this is not our last Father/Daughter getaway!"

She said, "Well, I just mean because I will be out of high school soon."

I said, "Okay, but I still plan on keeping up this tradition as best we can."

"Okay," she continued, "but it's my senior year, we should do something big."

"I agree," I said. "What is big?"

"We should go to Hawaii together over spring break!"

Whoa! That IS big. Immediately, I had three distinct thoughts, one after the other. First, I thought, "That is going to be expensive!"

Second, I thought, "I can't believe that my 17-year-old daughter wants to go to Hawaii with her dad on her senior year spring break. Wow! I am one lucky guy!" And third, I thought, "I am not missing this opportunity. We are going to Hawaii!"

At this time, I would like to officially and publicly thank my wife, Sharon, for being so gracious and willing to send us to Hawaii without her. She was a believer in what I was doing with Brittany, and she joyfully—or at least willingly—allowed us to go and make that investment. Sharon and I have had several great trips to Hawaii together, and it was certainly a sacrifice for her to watch us go without her. I was very grateful for her "sending" us.

I was almost giddy getting on that plane. I couldn't believe that I was going to such an extravagant and special place with my 17-year-old daughter. I was so pumped that, while I was certainly not perfect, I had somehow accomplished the goal I had set back when she was three years old. I told those girls at Gunderson High School that I really wanted to have a good relationship and be involved with Brittany when she was in high school. The last thing I wanted to do is repeat the all-too-common scenario of an absentee father with a daughter who wished her relationship with her dad were better. While all kinds of spring break trips were going on, with all sorts of crazy activities, I was actually heading to Hawaii with my daughter. I thought, "I am a blessed man." And I felt an appropriate amount of pride that, at least at some level, my plan to have a good relationship with my daughter had worked. She invited me to Hawaii! I wasn't awkwardly forcing some obligatory time with her. The trip was her idea, and I joyfully accepted her offer!

We had a blast running around Oahu. We stayed in Waikiki, with all its tourist stuff to do. We went shopping, ate in restaurants, and swam in the ocean. We drove our rental car over to the North Shore and swam at the famous Sunset Beach. We stopped in for a Dole Whip at the Pineapple Plantation. We snorkeled at Hanauma Bay, and took pictures with Diamond Head in the background. It was amazing.

The highlight, however, had to be accomplishing one of Brittany's lifelong dreams. She had always wanted to "swim with the dolphins." I did a little research, and found a place to do this in Oahu. I made reservations and got my camera ready. She had a blast getting in the water with the dolphins. She got to pet them, hold them and even give one a kiss. She gave them simple commands and thoroughly enjoyed the whole experience. My camera was clicking away, hoping to capture every possible moment.

Brittany swimming with the Dolphins on our Father/Daughter get away in Hawaii.

I look back on that afternoon with two strong feelings. The first feeling is how fun it was for Brittany to be able to do this. She was like a little kid, gushing over what was happening. The second feeling was how silly we ended up looking. When I told my friend Johnny about our experience, he laughed and called us "Dub-T," in a southern twang, while making a "T" sign with both hands. "Dub-T" was short for "WT," which stands for "White Trash." Johnny might have been onto something. At the very least, we were leaving a *trail* of white trash everywhere we went that day. Let me explain.

Brittany and I were traveling on a budget. It's not like a trip to Hawaii was a cheap proposition, after all. I'd purchased two plane tickets and reserved a hotel room on Waikiki. We went out to dinner each night, rented a car and paid for various trinkets along the way. So, Brittany and I had decided to cut costs where we could. For starters, we packed a lunch each day in a styrofoam cooler. The day Brittany swam with he dolphins was no different-except that our cheap cooler was now chipped and leaking little white balls wherever we walked.

We were not aware that this pending dolphin swim was at an extremely luxurious hotel—one of the nicest in Oahu. It was not normal for "guests" of this establishment to pack sack lunches or carry their own coolers, especially ones leaking little white balls. (Actually, a sack would have been an upgrade.) Our styrofoam cooler was a dead giveaway that we were indeed out of place. I set the cooler down and we enjoyed the dolphin experience. Then, the trouble started. After the dolphin swim, we were hungry. We found a very comfortable set of lounge chairs at this luxurious hotel, under a nice umbrella, where we could enjoy our lunch.

It didn't take long before a pool attendant noticed how much we stood out. He didn't use the term "Dub-T", but clearly he had some silent alarm sounding in his well-tanned head. He politely asked us if we were staying at the hotel (knowing that we were not), to which I proudly said, "No, we just swam with the dolphins!" I thought our purchase of a dolphin adventure would give us access to their private beach. But apparently the dolphin experience was owned by an outside company, not affiliated with the hotel. Therefore, the beach boy felt empowered to ask us to leave. He really didn't care if we swam with the dolphins or not. We got kicked out!

Begrudgingly, we grabbed our broken styrofoam cooler and our mismatched beach towels and got up and left in plain view of many. I think I was more mad than embarrassed. Either way, my friend loved calling us "Dub-T" for bringing our own lunch into the hotel and then getting kicked out. For Brittany and me, it was just another of the many great memories created by the Father/Daughter Getaway in Hawaii.

Lunch and a Trinket

The Father/Daughter Getaway turned into a life highlight and fabulous tradition. It gave us something to look forward to and something fun to do each year. However, I certainly wanted to do stuff with Brittany more than once a year. So, we started a little impromptu tradition we called, "Lunch and a Trinket." There was no prescribed frequency of this event, and it was usually spur of the moment. It was rather simple and something fun to do whenever the schedule permitted. I would invite her out to lunch, and then I'd buy her a simple little "trinket." This was not a pricy endeavor. It was not about spending much money. It was more about spending time and doing something fun. Lunch was simple. We might go to a fast food establishment or maybe to a sandwich shop. We would then go to a nearby store and pick up a simple toy or inexpensive piece of jewelry. The "trinket" would be something age-appropriate and fun. In the early years, it might be something from the Hello Kitty store. Then as she got older, it would be something a little more grown up. When I visited her in college, the trinket was some school supplies.

Again, this tradition was not about the "what," but more about the "who." The good thing about something like this is that not many dads are picking up their daughters from school and taking them out to lunch. And by "not many," I mean none. I gained points on this, because I stood out so much against all the other dads who were not making this effort. My desire was not to look good against other dads. My desire was to continue building a great relationship with my daughter. But, if I scored more points because of their lack of effort, so be it. We'll call that a bonus! This was a fun way to keep things consistently going with Brittany through the years. I wasn't waiting for the Father/Daughter Getaway to spend time with her. We now had a forming tradition that could happen at any time and at a moment's notice.

13th Year Video

I think I stole this idea from somebody, but I can't remember who. It sounded like such a great idea that it didn't take long to steal! As Brittany approached her 13th birthday, I wanted to do something special to mark this milestone. There are lots of definitions of what a woman is and many different opinions of when a girl "officially" becomes a woman. Is it a biological thing? A physical thing? An emotional thing? Is it when a girl enters or graduates high school? Is it when she gets married or perhaps when she has physical relations with a man? No one really knows when a young girl becomes a woman. I suppose an argument could be made for a little bit of all of the above playing a factor. In my mind, though, the 13th birthday was as good a milestone as any to pause and consider this important idea. While a 13 year-old is still, in many ways, immature, she is certainly in the process of leaving childhood and entering womanhood. A typical 13 year-old girl has started to develop into a woman physically as well as emotionally. She has probably started to wear a little make up as well as more mature clothing choices. At this time, things are definitely starting to change. So in our family, we chose to do something special to honor this birthday as the entrance into womanhood.

To celebrate, I contacted many of the women in our lives—women who loved Brittany and wanted the very best for her. I asked them if I could get them on video saying some words of wisdom, affirmation, and encouragement to Brittany on her 13th birthday. I spent a few weeks driving around the Bay Area in Northern California, filming these ladies giving their sage advice to Brittany as she was turning 13. In all, I had ten ladies who had watched Brittany grow up and loved her deeply. I filmed both grandmothers, aunts, cousins, good friends, and of course her own mom. Some of the ladies were strong Christians and spoke from that perspective, offering a Bible verse and encouragement from the Lord. Others did not speak from a faith perspective. However, all of them spoke from many years of experience and a deep desire for Brittany to grow up in a healthy way and make great choices. They shared their love and respect for her and their prayers for her future. There were plenty of tears as these older women wanted so much to communicate deep love, hope, and encouragement to Brittany at this critical time of her life. I edited the vignettes together and sprinkled in lots of video highlights of Brittany growing up. We presented the video to Brittany on her 13th birthday along with a blessing from both her parents. We let her know how proud we were of her and encouraged her in her life's direction thus far. We spoke into her life hopes, dreams and expectations as she entered adolescence. Our desire was to commemorate this birthday milestone with something significant. Our hope was to propel her into the next formative years of her life with a great blessing and encouragement to walk in a godly path toward womanhood. It was great! I wish every young girl had something similar. Sadly, too few ever receive a blessing and encouragement not only from their dads, but also from a larger community of women.

Half Birthdays

For years, my wife and I celebrated half birthdays with our kids. We started this tradition to give us the opportunity to take Brittany out on November 18th each year (her half birthday) and focus on her. The idea is to establish the date that is six months away from her actual birthday. In our family, Sharon and I take each kid on this day to the dinner location of their choice. We point out all of the positive traits and attributes we can think of. People can never hear enough encouragement and affirmation, and I think that's never truer than for a girl growing up through adolescence. We all know that the world is not sending out healthy encouragement and affirmation to our young girls.

After a great dinner filled with positive affirmation and encouragement, we buy one "birthday gift" for her. One-on-one time with our daughter, loads of encouragement and a present she's excited about—a great tradition indeed and something that has built into Brittany over the years.

None of the above is particularly genius or even all that original. However, I do believe these actions, along with the regular positive presence I strived for through Brittany's adolescence, combined to help her become all she could be. Brittany not only survived her adolescence, but she actually thrived during those tumultuous years. She did great in school and won many awards. She did great in athletics, achieving MVP status on her league champion high school volleyball team. And now, she is a productive young woman out in the workforce, achieving at a high level while volunteering in Young Life and helping our inner city ministries thrive. I could not be more proud of how she has turned out and what she is giving her life to.

More Dads

In the rest of this chapter, I will deliver several testimonies from dads who did it right. In my estimation, they have done great by their daughters. These are not young dads who are energetically working hard at trying to be a great dad. The dads below are veteran dads who have labored in this arena for at least 20 years. Their daughters are grown and doing well in life. They have all produced daughters who are awesome young women, who made it successfully through adolescence and are now making their way in the adult world. Of course, none of their daughters are perfect, and none of these dads would claim perfection, either.

The following are nonscientific, imperfect case studies on dads who seem to have figured something out, and their daughters have turned out well. Lean in and absorb these field-tested philosophies that have worked in the real world of raising daughters. These are not just ideas these dads hope to do some day and suspect will be good. These are ideas and philosophies that were carried out and deemed to have worked, through the benefit of 20/20 hindsight. The proof is in the pudding! These dads might not say they did a great job as fathers, but I am here to testify that their daughters are great! They are the kind of daughters that any young dad would hope to someday produce. You will notice some redundant themes. I left them in on purpose in order to highlight consistencies. I wish I had seen these ideas when I was starting to raise Brittany. Feel free to steal, tweak and take anything you read below. They are worthy of your theft! The following thoughts come from other dads and they are in their own words.

Stu

Okay, to be honest, I find this difficult, because I tend to see the things I haven't done well. I think the phrase "absentee fathers" is key. If you compile a great list of experiences, it won't make a hill of beans of a difference if you haven't had a consistent relationship over the long haul.

I'd say that my best parenting has come from listening to my wife—a female like my daughters—and trusting her instinct. Girls need very little "what to do" and much more "You are the greatest!" (Probably like most humans.) More encouragement, less praise. (Praise is for specific actions or behaviors, such as, "You got an A!" or "You scored a goal!" as opposed to encouragement, which is telling them how special they are for just being them, like, "You have such a great way you listen," or "I love the way you make friends with the outsider kids.")

My last thought: girls usually hear their fathers' voices at a volume of 11. We think we are being direct, but they hear anger or power. The voice of a father carries impact, so I know I need to be very aware of the way in which I communicate, otherwise it's all for naught, and I will be shut out or disqualified under the banner of "Dad doesn't get it."

One thing I did well was take my daughters on trips. Here are two:

Trip 1

The first trip I took each of my girls on was when they were 13 years old. We went wherever they wanted to go in the USA. Of my three daughters, one wanted to go to Los Angeles, one to New York City, and one to Victoria Island. On these trips, we set out to do whatever the girls wanted to do, see shows, stay in a castle, etc. I wanted

Stu and Claire enjoying a formal tea on their
"13-year-old" trip

to show them how they should be treated by a man on a date, so we enjoyed nice dinners, "high tea," and so on. I also bought them each a memorable piece of jewelry. I never do that, so it was really special. For example, we were walking the streets of NYC, and we came to Tiffany's jewelry store.

Hannah's eyes lit up, because she knew what it was. Tiffany's has four stories, and we were greeted by the doorman in a tux. I whispered to the first salesperson, "My daughter has turned 13, and I need the cheapest thing in your store!" She said aloud, "What a special day! We have lovely Tiffany's heart necklaces on the 4th floor, back left counter!" ($99) Hannah loved it. What a memory! The packaging, the blue bag, walking the streets of NYC, eating on street corners, shopping at knock-off underground NY stores, staying in a friend's 300-square-foot flat in Soho—it was all part of this special time together.

Trip 2

High school senior year, we took a dad/daughter trip to Africa. I pulled them out of school and traveled to Africa for a month. Not "hotel Africa," but "dirt floor Africa." I pulled them out of school because in their senior year, they are really done anyway. I had to fight with the administration a bit, but they couldn't disagree that the experience was worth more than the school they missed. The time was priceless! Thirty days alone with my daughter, seeing the needy of the world. We also did a bit of fun stuff on the way, but 80 percent was visiting the poor, staying with people doing remarkable work, and giving our lives to the "least of these."

These trips have varied a bit. Kayla's was about 35 days, and Hannah's was only ten days. This was because Hannah was more sensitive to missing school, and because different opportunities came up that allowed the different trips. Hannah's time included days in London, but Kayla's didn't.

These times were amazing because we talked about the things we saw, as well as life in general. My daughters were about to leave for college, and I had this unbelievable time to connect with each of them for a chunk of time. We traveled as friends, not father and daughter, because after all, they were 18!

It's easy for dads to say, "Oh I couldn't do that," "I don't get that much vacation," "That's too much money," or "My daughter can't miss school." To all those things I say, "BS." You are men, and you do whatever you want most of the time. Take out a loan. Take a leave from your job. I'd take a second mortgage on the house, for the experience these trips have given to us as dad and daughter. (Mom is actually a bit jealous, because of the special memories we made.)

I also don't think this trip has the same power if you do it with the whole family. I don't think missing school is mandatory, but I do think it adds a bunch because your daughter's friends know about it and are excited for her. Plus, she'll hear tons of, "I wish my dad would do that," "You have a cool dad," etc. Your daughter gets to hear from their friends that their dad loves them!

Marty

Here are the things I did millions of times as our girls grew up.

Often, when they were young, they received these things easily. As they got older, it was, at times, a cool reception. But their response did not matter. I was always building up a spiritual and emotional bank account for future cultural "withdrawals."

I said, "I love you" to them often.

I said, "I am proud of you" often.

I said, "You are beautiful inside and out" often.

I lived my life to earn and keep their trust. Daily decisions and life decisions.

I let them continually figure out their faith by "examining" my wife's and mine.

Kids pick up faith by what they observe more than what they are told.

I counted my own experience of Jesus as the most important gift I could give them.

I counted my love for my wife as the second most important gift I could give them.

I tried to maintain as many corny jokes and punch lines as possible.

I tried to plan fun, short, cheap vacations. It is what we could afford.

I thanked God for their lives often and knew each day was a gift.

I still do most of these things. Our oldest is 30, married and has two kids. We see their family often. Our baby is 24, has a good job, works as a Young Life College volunteer and has a great church. She lives close, too. We know we are blessed.

None of what we did worked. Everything we did worked. The mystery is the journey. Love not only covers a multitude of sins, but it also covers a multitude of things I did poorly as a dad.

Gary

As I reflect, I'm reminded that the result of my fundamental beliefs and commitments don't always produce what I had hoped for, mostly because I'm a knucklehead.

Our three daughters came a little later than most. This was very helpful for me, because I had grown up a bit more and was ready for them, or so I thought.

I had a very strong awareness that these girls were a gift from God for me to shape with His guidance. I remember lifting each crying newborn up to the Lord with thanksgiving and gratitude. I embraced their uniqueness from day one. I have enjoyed each little person's individual differences so much. I always think about them separately. I crafted special dates, gifts, travel or special trips to fit each kid's interests. I think they each knew they had their own special part of my heart.

I always whispered or shouted to them how beautifully they were made by God for His purposes. I organized special evenings where we might just honor one daughter. It allowed us all to reflect upon the uniqueness present in each. I always mixed humor and laughter with the girls. I remember being in Moscow, where we lived for several years, playing soccer in the fall blizzard season. It was one of those games that Katie made a great kick and I screamed out, "Katie, your foot hit the ball!" All the parents thought I was a jerk, but Katie and I laughed our butts off. The point is, each daughter loved knowing that they were loved at a very deep level.

An epic picture of Gary and Katie on her wedding day.

I always made a big deal of the idea of building memories. Almost everything we've done left some mark on them. I took one of the girls on each of my work trips. We had a rotation, and each one knew whose turn it was, and who was on deck. On one trip to a Young Life camp north of St. Petersburg during the winter, we were traveling on the last train of the night to a very remote village. We got off the train one village early, at 1:00 AM in the morning. It was minus 16 and snowing. So, I carried Hannah on my back for two miles, with my luggage in my hands. We finally arrived, thawed out, and had a great weekend.

I have hundreds of those stories. The point is that each daughter always felt integrated in my work and the task of following Christ.

I always tried to love my wife well, but like most men, I failed at times. Whenever I really screwed up, I made sure that they knew I apologized and that I loved their mother, and that she is the best. Again, this is a little hard to write because I have blown it a bunch.

Here is what I am most thankful for: when each of my daughters were young, they said something like, "Daddy, when you are done with Mommy, will you marry me?" Isn't that great? It always made me laugh. I wish all little girls had a chance to have a daddy that they would be loved by and that they knew loved their mommy.

Roy

A girl faces incredible challenges that guys like us never see or understand. There are countless things that can tear at a girl's confidence, and our society seems to throw all of them at adolescent girls. It scars them and makes them cautious as they become adults. It can make them long for acceptance and seek love in the wrong ways. I wanted to raise a daughter with the strength to stand up to all of that.

So, I focused on loving her. But we all aim to love our kids, so what did I do to specifically love her? Several things:

> I was present in her life—from sporting events to dance recitals, from school open houses to taking her to church on Sundays. This let her know that I valued her. Having a dad around who seemed so huge and so capable in her little eyes, gave her the confidence to say "no" when she needed to.

I talked to her. I shared stories about my life and asked questions about hers. She not only learned from this, but she grew comfortable with herself in the process.

I said more than just, "I love you." Those are simple and important words, but daughters also need to hear, "You are the best . . . you are amazing . . . you are gorgeous . . . you are special." Words matter, and young girls need to hear the right words.

I honored her mother. I once read that the best way a man can show his love for his kids is to love their mother. So my daughter never heard a cross word from me about her mother. Instead, she saw me honor her mother, serve her, romance her, and always act like a gentleman toward her. I put her mother on a pedestal and acted like I adored her (even when I might not feel that way). It modeled how a man should treat a woman and it gave my daughter the guidelines to understand when a man crosses the line.

I wasn't perfect. I made mistakes. But that's true of everything in life. The key to raising a daughter is to not give up and to always let her know that she is loved.

Richard

I try to view life in general as not a very complicated process, which is how I view raising kids—boys or girls. Parents have been doing it for thousands of years and in general there is only a small percentage of bad apples. So how tough can it be? Give them food, shelter, clothes, time, love, discipline, and an example of how someone should live in this world, with the understanding that Jesus exists and has overcome the world, and kids will generally turn out fine with a healthy perspective.

Richard and Steph with an emotional Father/ Daughter dance
Photo credit to @TheYoungrens

I am not a man of many words, so I won't use many here as I describe what we did and didn't do:

We tried to be their parents, and not their best friends.

We surrounded ourselves with friends that we respected, which provided many examples for the girls. (Our five closest couple friends are believers and have been married over 20 years each, and have strong healthy relationships.)

I loved their mother with all my heart and all my soul.

I loved God with all my heart and all my soul.

We made our home a safe place for them.

I met the boyfriends before they went out, not to intimidate but to make sure they understood that the girls had a father that loved and cared for them. If my physical presence intimidated them, then that was just a bonus.

We didn't treat the girls as princesses, as if they could do no wrong. We called them on it when they did do something wrong.

I give away my time, talents and treasures. (Steph was four when we started taking her with us to feed the homeless.)

I teased them . . . a lot.

We laughed . . . a lot.

I let them know that I would literally lay my life down for them.

RJ

As our two girls were growing up, a tradition began most Sundays after church: a Daddy Adventure. It was my job to do something of my choice with the whole family. It was a surprise each week. Sometimes it was as simple as where we would go out to eat, and other times it involved dressing a certain way in preparation. But always a surprise!

On Daddy Adventures, we went to the zoo, Carl's Jr. to eat, a museum, a drive-in, the mountains and a picnic in the park. One time I announced a Daddy Adventure after church and started driving. The girls started guessing where we were headed. They believed we were headed to Grandma J's house in San Jose. When we passed her exit, the guessing went into high gear. After an hour or two, I pulled out my Mickey Mouse ears and a trip to Disneyland was on!

As the years passed and their lives became more complicated, we did fewer and fewer Daddy Adventures. However, when my oldest daughter was about to turn 16, we asked her what she wanted for her sweet sixteen birthday. Her reply surprised us. She said, "All I want is a Daddy Adventure." Well, I gave her a packing list and told her to be in the car at 5:30 in the morning. We drove to San Francisco airport, got on a plane, and she flew with me on a business trip to Hawaii.

These trips did a couple of things as I look back. First, they made me fun. They made me a trusted leader. They made life an adventure. All these things translated to their Father in heaven. He is fun. He is trusted leader, and His life is an adventure!

Darrell

Having five kids, two of whom were daughters, I quickly realized that each one of them needed different things in a relationship with me. Finding out what this was with my daughters was harder for me than it was with the boys, most likely because I'd do things with the boys that I liked to do as I was growing up. Not so much with daughters. Also, one of my daughters was with my former wife, which added to the challenges. The following are few things I did that helped me with our relationship:

Pray: Seeking God's wisdom was and is very powerful with what I did and said. Only God understands what they are going through and what they need from their dads.

Communication: Very easy to say, and for us dads it's easy to think we are communicating. But often I found that my daughter was not willing to open up about issues. Communication, for me, was mostly just listening, not trying to fix it or get her to see it my way. The more I listened, the more she asked me what I thought.

Spending time: I found the more time we had alone, the better our relationship became. Doing something alone with them was the best thing we did. A trip to pick up ice cream or coffee, out buying mom's gifts, going to get tires rotated, etc. It did not matter why we were together. What was important was that we were together.

Love them unconditionally: I think this was one of the biggest things I worked at letting them know. Regardless of what they said or did, I loved them.

I would love to tell you that this is a perfect model to follow. Over the 30 plus years of raising kids, there were many bumps along the way. At times it was hard to just let go and trust that God would protect them and even restore a broken line of communication. Knowing all I know now, I would not change one thing, because my relationship grew with my kids—especially my daughters—and so did my trust in God.

Kevin

A few thoughts . . .

Be parents of "YES." We found ourselves too naturally and too quickly saying "no" to our kids when they asked for stuff. "Can Jenny sleep over?" "Can I have a snack?" "Can we build a pillow fort?" "Can we . . . ?" "Can I . . . ?" Our response was "no" only because it was a tad inconvenient. That's lousy! So we decided to be parents of "YES." We would respond to their requests more thoughtfully. If our reason to say "no" was out of inconvenience, then that was unacceptable! We started saying "yes" a lot. Then as they grew up and needed to "individuate" and push against us, we had already built a foundation between us (parents and kids) where they knew we were "for" them, and wanted the best for them. They had little to push against. They knew that when we did say "no" that it was a thoughtful and reasonable response.

With regard to television, we watched TV with them. We didn't use TV as a babysitter. (Bad idea to let cartoons raise your kids!) When inappropriate stuff inadvertently came on, we didn't ignore it.

We talked about it. If they weren't free to talk about stuff with us, then who were they going to talk about weird, difficult stuff with? So, as awkward as it would be, we would turn off the TV and discuss the topic. Our mantra was, "We don't get our moral values—our sense of right and wrong—from TV and movies!"

Another big deal was when Erin was in middle school. I read a book called *What Kids Need Most in a Dad*. Most eye-opening was a section of questions in the middle of the book. It challenged my relationship with my kids. They said that a good dad knew the answer to these questions. I didn't. It was questions (around 70 questions!) like, "When you first wake up in the morning how do you feel about yourself?" "What is your greatest fear?" "What is your biggest dream?" I knew how the kids would answer some of them, but not most! That startled me into doing something, so I planned a trip with just Erin and I. We drove down to Magic Mountain. The whole drive down, and while we were waiting in line, and as we drove home, I'd tell Erin to pick a number. Then I would ask the corresponding question from the book. It was amazing, and it's one of our favorite memories together. I grew to know so much more about my baby.

Clif

The most important place to start is to love their mother first and foremost. The girls always knew that their mother was the delight of my life. Their model of what they believe about male female relationships starts here. If their picture is a healthy one, then they have the expectation of being treated that way by young men. When a guy doesn't do that, it sends a clear signal that something is not right.

Girls need to hear Dad tell Mom, "I love you." They need to see Dad kiss Mom and put his arm around her. They should see Dad hug Mom often. We had a regular date night, even if in the early days all we could afford was to get something to drink. Marilyn and I tried to get a weekend away occasionally without the girls. They understood that we saw our relationship as a priority.

It's also important for a dad to date his daughters. I can't remember if I had a specific age, but by the time they were eight years old, I took each of the girls out every 4-6 weeks for breakfast or an ice cream cone. We would talk about their world, and my job was to love them and listen. The key was being together as dad and daughter. As they got older, we had more time to talk about their friends, school, the Lord, and young men. I always opened the door for them, tried to listen well, and as time went along, listened for the places when they wanted to talk. But my goal was to give them an example of how a young man should also treat them.

I had a "fun" tradition that all the girls understood before they went out on an official date with a guy. (Sixteen years-old was the earliest age it could ever happen.) At least it was fun for me—maybe frightening for a boy. If a guy asked one of my girls out on a date and I thought there was any chance we would allow it, I had "The Talk" with him. The girls would die a thousand deaths when I said it needed to happen, but that was the standard operating procedure, and guys understood it.

I would take the would-be suitor out for lunch or an ice cream and try to be as friendly and engaged as possible. At some point, I'd say something like this: "(Boy's name), we have enjoyed having you around our family and getting to know you. I understand from (one of my daughters' names) that you want to take her to the dance next weekend. You have been around our family and seen the values that are important to us. You know how important faith is to us. I want you to know that I expect you to uphold our family values when you are on a date.

The world normally says that the girl sets limits, but I expect you to give good leadership in this area, and to uphold the highest moral standards. My daughter is responsible for her actions, but I also expect you to be honorable in every way."

Later in life, all of the girls said that, as much as they hated this little tradition, they felt very safe. They loved that Dad protected them.

Michael

I have two daughters, ages 20 and 16, and I am their biggest fan. I work hard to make sure they know that. How do I make sure they know? I am at almost every event they are involved in, whether it is sports, music, or an academic event. In a world where kids are ignored, forgotten, & slip into the crowd, I call out my girls' names regularly. I call them, text them, and Facebook message them to send positive, encouraging words to them whenever I can.

I praise them regularly. Not in a fake way, but a consistent way. I truly believe that my girls need to hear five positive messages for every corrective message. That ratio gives me the right to be truthful and direct when needed, while being corrective. It also builds up their confidence as young ladies.

I open the door for them whenever I can. I serve them whenever I can. I constantly check in to see what they need. I accept them where they are and encourage them to think big and shoot for the stars. I remind them that they were made for a purpose and they need to find what that purpose is. I also gently remind them that they were created by a loving God, and He really is the one to help them figure out their purpose and reason for being.

Finally, I love their mom. They see me opening the door for her, treating her special, and deferring to her whenever possible. I serve their mom and treat her as an equal partner. I want them to look for a man who will treat them with respect, and love them as Christ loves the Church.

Grant

One tradition that my daughter Allison and I established early on was a "father/daughter date." The idea behind this was to demonstrate to Allison just how special she was to me. Sometimes, I would surprise her with an activity that I knew she would enjoy. Other times, I would ask her what she would like to do and we would plan it together. The activity or event really didn't matter all that much. It was just an excuse for us to be together and for her to have my undivided attention.

Our first date was to see an evening showing of the movie *The Secret Garden*. She got all dressed up in her red dress, white tights, and shiny black shoes. Her mother and older brother made a big deal as the two of us left to go to the movie theater. Once there, we got popcorn and drinks and settled in our seats to watch the movie. During one dramatic scene, the choral voices soared with the background music, and I heard Allison give a little gasp. Then, with an innocence and wonder that only a four year old can possess, she exclaimed in a hushed whisper, "Daddy! Angels!" To her, the faceless singing voices we heard could only mean one thing—angels! The gift for me that night was to catch a glimpse of the way that my daughter viewed the world. The challenge for me as a father was to make sure that her view of the world could remain one of innocence and wonder for as long as possible.

Every so often, we would have an overnight event. One of those times, we stayed at a friend's cabin near Santa Cruz. That evening, we went to the Boardwalk and rode rides and played games. Afterwards, we had a late night snack at Denny's. We topped off the evening by coming back to the cabin and watching a rented movie together. Allison still has the little stuffed animal that I won for her that night at the Boardwalk and we still watch movies together for special bonding times.

John

It's hard to think back to a million moments and isolate effectiveness. I'd say that it's more about an attitude towards your daughters.

First, figure out how to like them as they are. I think we lay a heavy load on our kids when we have a strong inclination that they reflect who we are. Then, when they misbehave, throw a tantrum, or act rudely, we are threatened and act out of that as parents. Our kids aren't reflections of us. First and foremost, they are unique creations. Sometimes, as a "pleaser," I wanted them to be built more like me, but they weren't. My kids actually aren't as affected by others' opinions. That made them less friendly when they were little, and less driven to become well-liked and widely-liked.

Next, daughters need to know that they are the second most important thing in your life behind your own relationship with Christ and alongside their mother. We can talk faith until we are blue in the face, but when they see little moments—not the dramatic ones—of your first love of Jesus, your times of true faith stick with them forever. When they see your acts of kindness; reading the Word; praying; the way you apologize; saying I love you; seeking justice for the poor; being generous; being gracious . . . that is discipleship for your kids.

And last, it's all by grace, I believe. We are all faulty. Apologies are hard but powerful. Pray, be wrong occasionally, be human before them and not a fake icon. Love them, even when you get nothing in return (like your Father in heaven). Be absolutely committed to loving them.

Brent

I wanted my girls to enjoy sports (like their dad) so I figured I would show them "older girls" who were successful in different sports.

I took them to high school and college softball, basketball, and soccer games. We always got lunch (food is always very important and I let them pick the meal) and we had fun at the games. Every now and then, we would hang around to get autographs, and the girls are always much nicer than the guys. This allowed my daughters to see other girls playing sports, and it gave them an interest as well. Both my girls played college soccer, but more importantly, the mutual love of sports is something that helped us build an even stronger bond in our relationship. Whether it's going to a game, or watching football together, just spending time with your daughters is building a stronger relationship. My daughters now love football, baseball, and hockey as much as I do.

On the left, Brent holds Courtney before one of HIS games. On the right, Brent holds Courtney after one of HER games. He led the 49ers to three Super Bowls and she led the UNC Tar Heels to an NCAA division 1 women's soccer Championship.

Sports really built confidence and self-esteem, first and foremost. The lessons they learned by being part of a team are so valuable to young women, especially when it comes to communication and problem-solving among their peers.

Steve

My daughters always knew that they were unconditionally loved. I demonstrated this to them through my actions and my words. My "love language" is physical touch, so I am constantly giving my kids hugs—even big bear hugs. They also say that I showed them that they were a priority in my life by being involved in their activities, either through coaching, tutoring, or just cheering from the sidelines. I am also a big teaser, so they were subjected to loving teasing. They also quickly learned to dish it back and I let them know that they were really good at it. However, Christy and I were very purposeful to teach our girls proper biblical respect for us, one another and those in authority. I always stopped what I was doing to listen to them, even when I was working toward a deadline on a project. This has kept the lines of communication open even through the teenage years. I also admitted to the girls when I was wrong and asked for their forgiveness if it affected them.

Mark

Mark, Katie and Laura

Be there!

LISTEN, then LISTEN some more, and then LISTEN some more. I can't say I always did this, because the tendency is to listen too little and give advice too quickly.

Love unconditionally, even when she screws up.

Love your wife and let her see that model.

Get involved with what she likes (school, church, cheer, sports, choir, reading, etc.).

Love her friends, but don't be nosy.

Challenge her to figure out what she loves and then support her in that.

Again, let her see you model a good marriage. Love your wife!

Talk to her about boys as she enters those teen years. Most important is not what they say or look like, but how they act and what they do. Actions speak much louder than words.

Model your faith. Acting out your faith in daily life is much more important than preaching your faith.

Even though you want to give her everything, don't! She's got to earn it and work for it.

She is going to enter the secular working world and have to "play hardball with the boys," so make sure she is ready and able.

Mike

First of all, the best thing I did for all my kids, was love God. It is so hard to be a good father without knowing the Heavenly Father. I am constantly growing as a man and as a father by putting Christ first in my life. Apart from being a pastor, my children knew that I loved the word of God, and that it is a huge part of my life. When you are in God's word you are constantly reminded that it is both possible to change (by God's grace) and in what ways you need to change (specific instruction from the principles in God's word) and the necessity of change (the word of God is a mirror for your soul).

Secondly, I was a better father when I was a better husband. The second best thing we can do for their children is to love their mother.

We cherished our kids, but we did not want to communicate to them the whole world revolved around them. They were more secure in our love for them when they saw our love for each other.

Thirdly, I have grown more convinced over the years about the value of the local church. Churches are different in many ways—some are more "successful" in numbers and more "gifted" in staff and ministries, but a healthy, Christ-centered church is the best "village" to raise a child. Cindy and our children had the opportunity to be spiritually nurtured in a multi-generational way as they grew up in church. People praying for them, teaching them, encouraging them, crying and laughing with them, correcting them, serving with them, and simply loving them.

There are many things I could write about—many things I can look back at and know I could have done better—but I will throw this out as a lesson I had to learn. In her temperament, Cindy is more like her father than my sons are. This was a challenge just in itself. Sometimes I thought I was talking to myself in the ways we would discuss (debate) issues. I have learned that I can show her my love for her in a real way when I don't have to WIN the argument now, but just listen to her and value her opinion.

Scud

I made a conscious effort to listen as much as I could to whatever my daughters wanted to talk about. I wanted to be present and focus on them when they wanted that. It was on their terms, and I tried to be available when the opportunities presented themselves.

I tried to verbalize my love as often as possible, but worked at backing that up more with actions than words. It was almost like earning the right to be heard by my daughters and really doing contact work—not with ulterior motives, but simply to demonstrate my love. This took all forms, small and big. It began when they were very young, with making it a priority to attend any elementary school assembly where they were recognized, all types of sporting events, father-daughter dances in high school, movie dates, dinner dates, musical concerts, church plays, Giants' games dates . . . any and everything took priority in my schedule. I tried to look at their interests and figure out what we could do together. Our daughter Katie was into basketball for a number of years, and dreamed of playing at Stanford, so I took her to several Stanford women's games.

I spent a lot of time listening, many times late at night over the phone, but in person as well. When our daughter Kristi was in college, I think we averaged at least one phone call a week talking about her major and why she wanted to change it that week. Most of those were late at night because she knew that was when she could reach me and I was available. Katie carried on that tradition because she saw it happen with Kristi. It was key for me to demonstrate that to Katie as well.

We laughed a lot. I made it a point to be silly with them so they could laugh at me. I tried to always treat them and speak to them respectfully. I was probably guilty of speaking to them on a level of maturity that they may not have reached yet, but I think that communicated to them that I expected them to be mature and grow into that. I think treating them with honor through my language helped them to develop a healthy self-confidence and respect for themselves.

My life and schedule were often full of many commitments with most associated with the ministry, so when I made them and their events and lives a priority I think it communicated how valuable they were to me, as well as subconsciously causing them to believe in their own value as a person. I think this gave them a basis to make good decisions about their lives and relationships.

Katie, Scud and Kristi enjoying Hawaii

I also worked at showing them my love for my wife Missy and her priority in my life. I demonstrated that love and priority in how I treated Missy and how I would not allow them to treat her. It was often little things around the house such as emptying the dishwasher, because Missy hates to do that. Or doing the dishes after dinner because that showed that we shared in the household duties. Or encouraging Missy to have time away with friends. All of these things communicated my sincere love for Missy, and created a sense of safety and comfort within our home that they often did not see in the homes of their friends.

JC

I tried to help with the driving to and from all of our daughter Annalise's activities. Sometimes it was just the two of us, and sometimes it was a car full of her friends. There was always conversation, usually pretty surface level, but once in a while it got deep and personal. There was a great deal of driving during the middle school years because we moved and wanted to keep Annalise in the school she attended, so that meant we had to take her and pick her up every day. It helped that my schedule was flexible so I could do this, especially picking her up from school. I got to hear about the day and help her get ready for whatever activity she had after school.

Because of my schedule, I became the dad who took Annalise and her friends to the midnight showings of the *Harry Potter* movies. This became a tradition for the years before Annalise could drive. After Annalise got her driver's license, I got a great deal of time back because I didn't have to take her everywhere, but I missed the time with her in the car.

Alan's Summary

Aren't these dads great examples? They are real dads with real daughters, who have taken their role as father of a daughter seriously. They have intentionally formed traditions with their girls, and they've invested in and successfully raised great daughters. Let's listen to them, because their stories serve as great examples of real life dads who have climbed the mountain and are now showing us the way. As you reflect on these dads, make sure you understand the "why" and that will inform the "what" of their actions. In other words, don't be discouraged by some of the extraordinary flexibility some of these dads had in their schedules. Likewise, don't be scared off by the amounts of money that some of them seemed to spend. You can accomplish great things with whatever time and resources you have to spend. I wish I had seen this content when I was just getting started. I would have stolen many of their ideas.

I heard this from these dads:

Take your daughters on trips.

Make things fun.

Love your wife.

Model your faith in Jesus.

Work hard to be trustworthy.

Say "I love you" often.

Be spontaneous.

Be a leader.

Form traditions.

Create memories.

Have your own authentic faith.

Apologize.

Pray.

Be vulnerable.

Be thankful.

Be present.

Honor your wife.

Be their parent, not their best friend.

Meet their boyfriends.

Intimidation is a bonus.

Love God and their mother with all your heart and soul.

Take your daughters on adventures.

Don't avoid inappropriate stuff.

Talk through it.

Take their call when you are in a meeting.

Get to know their friends.

Let them see you be affectionate with their mother.

Give five positive messages for every one corrective.

Initiate communication often.

Let them see you live out your faith.

Make sure they know they are the second most important thing in your life.

Value church.

Give big bear hugs.

Date your daughter.

Don't tell them what to do as much as listen carefully and ask questions.

Do the dishes.

Real Talk

"If there is one thing that I can tell dads, it is to be PRESENT in your daughter's life. As a girl, I can tell you that we long to be loved and valued, and in a world that thinks being "perfect" is everything and what you look like defines who you are, it is critical that us girls find our affirmation and validation in the right places."

"Ever since I was a little girl, my father has set aside intentional time to spend with me—time that remained uninterrupted by work, friends, telephones and outsiders. Quality time means something special to girls, and those memories are strong reminders of moments that my father chose me over everybody else. His pursuit of me continued to manifest in countless sacrifices, showing me that my needs took value over his wants at any given moment. I have never seen someone give as sacrificially as my dad, and I have never gone without anything I've needed thanks to his willingness to lay himself down before me."

Chapter 7

Do This!

Testimonies from girls who made it and had dads who loved them well

Throughout this book, I hope to blend a good mix of ideas, philosophy, personal testimony, and best practices from a number of different perspectives. My hope is that dads with daughters will be inspired to live differently and love their daughters more effectively. This chapter might prove to be the most helpful, inspiring, and profound of all. In this chapter, I have gathered a number of testimonies from different women who have survived. More than just survived, they have thrived. These are girls of various ages who have great relationships with their dads, and who claim that this great relationship made a huge difference in their lives.

The women in this section represent the "after" group in the "before and after" of girls who were loved well and turned out great. These girls are the kind of girls you'd be proud to have your daughter turn out to be like. They are happy, productive, wholesome, winsome women of faith and love in their post-teenage years. This group is comprised of single women, some married and some married with children. The ages range from college students and beyond. Once again, no one here is claiming perfection, but these ladies are going on record as saying that their dad "did it well," and that being loved well by their dad has given them a huge advantage in life. Listen to their stories and learn from their dads. In short, do this! Again, each excerpt is written by the young women whose names appear at its beginning.

Kristi

I could not have had a better father. He's a dad that never made it difficult to believe in God because he was such an amazing father to my siblings and me. He made it easy for me to make the transition to a heavenly Father who would send His Son to die for me. My dad was invested and verbal about his affection for both my mom and me. He loved and disciplined me and I never doubted his unconditional love for me. It allowed me to make good decisions in my life. I never needed additional male attention (besides the regular girl stuff) because I was so certain my dad, who said I was amazing, was telling me the truth. My self-confidence was always high. I have had good, healthy relationships with males, both friends and boyfriends. I was able to save my virginity for marriage because I was so confident in who I was, in my dad's love, and in my heavenly Dad's plan that was best for me. My dad is my hero and one of the hardest transitions in my life was making my husband the top man in my life over my dad. That's how good he was! I could not have been more blessed.

Karli

A few years ago on a Sunday morning, my mom was desperately trying to rush me out the door to make it to church on time. My dad told her not to worry—that she should go and grab seats and that he and I would leave a few minutes later and meet her there. To my surprise, as soon as my mom closed the door behind her, my dad told me to put on my bathing suit and pack some sunscreen—we were taking a spontaneous day trip to the beach! I had no idea that my parents had planned a fun Father/Daughter day and made it look spontaneous. We laughed as we drove the opposite way from church and I wondered what mom would think. Now, skipping out on church on Sunday is not necessarily a good thing, but that Sunday I felt like the luckiest girl in the world to have such an awesome dad and to get to spend the day with him hanging on the beach.

Having my dad always present in my life, always encouraging me, always protecting me, and always teaching me has had the greatest impact in shaping the young woman I am today. He has always led by example—showing his joy for the Lord by singing praises early in the morning and showing his love for his wife and all his daughters every day. Having my dad involved in my life has always motivated me to be better. He was there for every soccer game, gymnastics meet, dance performance, and football game that he could come to. As a young girl—it means so much to have your father there for you. My dad is always pushing me to be the best I can be and reminding me to stay positive and keep a good attitude. His presence gets me excited and pumped to perform well in all my endeavors.

My dad's active pursuit of maintaining a loving marriage with my mom and his involvement in my life, has had a huge impact on how I view relationships and dating. My dad has always been very honest with me about the men that he thinks are suitable to date—and even more honest about the unsuitable men in my life. Whenever I'd bring a guy friend over in high school, his first words to them were always, "Are you interested in dating my daughter?" and quickly followed by a stern, "Do you love Jesus?" and then, "How are your grades in school?" So embarrassing at the time, but 100% appreciated at this stage in my life. My dad has taken it upon himself to have a few awkward conversations with me when he felt that I was struggling with a relationship or dating someone that he did not think was a good fit. I have always valued my dad's opinion and his words have greatly influenced the ways that I have interacted with past boyfriends and current relationships with guys. It means so much to me that my dad reaches out and talks to me about the sometimes-awkward things. He even shares stories of his dating history, which generally provide a little comic relief to the situation. I look at other girls my age (college), some of which do not have great father-daughter relationships and judging by the way they treat themselves and relationships with boys I feel extremely blessed to have grown up with a loving father. I feel that my dad's love gave me security and confidence in myself that has kept me grounded and kept me from making a lot of really poor choices.

It has always been my dad's dream to hike the John Muir Trail with his kids. One summer, my older sister and I were somehow free to leave our lives in North Carolina to backpack for two weeks with our dad. I couldn't believe it, but I was committed to spending two weeks with no technology, walking up mountains with a heavy pack on my back, and sleeping in a tent with my father every night. I had no clue what I had gotten myself into.

*Rich and Karli resting during their big hike on the
John Muir trail*

The trip was intense. Painful blisters, sore feet, mosquito bites, sunburns, bear scares, freezing "showers," and stinky, stinky clothes. It was quite the adventure, and to this day the coolest thing my dad has ever talked me into. I have never spent so much quality time with my dad in my life, and I wouldn't trade that time with him for anything. We played cards in the tent every night and talked about anything and everything! I got to hear funny stories about his mistakes growing up and about the milestones in his life. My sister and I got to share all of our opinions, thoughts, and ideas with him.

My dad and I had a good relationship before the hike, but that bonding time on the trail made me appreciate my relationship with him in new ways. We hang out more, joke and laugh more, and even talk about the harder things a lot easier. I'm not saying that every dad needs to take his daughters on intense wilderness adventures to have a great relationship. But I would say that we girls need our fathers actively participating in our lives. We need our dads at every competition, soccer game, and dance performance he can come to. We need him to treat us like princesses, but not spoil us rotten. We need him to take us out of school for surprise day trips to the beach. We need him to be hard on the boys that don't deserve us, and always push us to be our best. We need him to remind us that he loves us every day and to be joyful and thankful and excited for life.

Nobody is perfect, and every father-daughter relationship has its ups and downs. What is important is to always be there, and show us love in whatever ways a dad can. Even if we don't appreciate it in our teenage years, we will learn just how much a father's loving relationship means, and how important it is for us girls to make it through those troublesome adolescent years.

Lizzy

My dad is a man of few words. Constantly telling me how proud he is, how much he loves me, and how he's always there for me isn't really his style. And it doesn't have to be.

Regardless of the words that have been used throughout my lifetime, or more accurately haven't been used, those same messages have always been successfully sent and clearly received. So how did the big guy do it? I've been thinking about that a lot lately, and I've come up with what must have been his secret four-part strategy.

1. He engaged instead of doting.

My dad's style of showing love has always included a heavy dose of teasing and games that ended with the loser eating a packet of Taco Bell mild sauce. I wasn't treated like a princess, and I'm so thankful for that. Instead, I got to participate in crazy fun with my dad and that's built the foundation for a great relationship with a dad I actually enjoy spending time with.

2. He showed up even when it was painful.

My sister and I both played soccer for 16 years. It's a sport that requires spending weekend after weekend at tournaments in the middle of nowhere and it also happens to be a sport my dad can't stand. Nevertheless, he was out there at soccer tournaments after a 60-hour workweek with his camping chair and his basketball analogies. And when I was scared of the ball, he was out in the backyard kicking soccer balls at me. Yes, at me. Did I mention he has a unique way of showing love?

3. He cares for me like only a dad can.

He may not be a man of many words—he may challenge me, tease me, and kick soccer balls at me—but that's all perfectly balanced by the meaningful ways that he shows me he cares. Little things, like the way he calls me "Booger" (endearing term in his book), the way he brought me (an awkward teen) flowers on Valentine's Day, with a card that said "If you ever need a Valentine, I'll be your stand in."

4. He earned my utmost respect.

My dad is probably the last person in the world that I would ever want to disappoint. The reason for this is simply that I respect him so much. He works harder than anyone I know, loves his family, loves Jesus, adopts our friends as family, gives his time to the church and is more generous than anyone I know. Because of the respect I have for my dad, I have never been too cool for him, can never learn enough from him and will always be challenged to be more and more like him. I'm the luckiest girl to have him as my dad and one day my kids will be lucky to have him as a grandpa!

Robyn

While some might consider "Daddy's Girl" a derogatory phrase, I hold it in high esteem and am proud to say I am one of them. Though I never aspired to grow up to be a lawyer like my dad, I emulated him in almost every other way possible, from his personality to his personal preferences to his sense of humor. I think one reason for this is that we were already very similar to start with, but also his amazing "dad" skills made me want to grow up to be like him He set the bar high for every man in my life.

Looking back, I can see more clearly the "how" of my dad's parenting style than I could when I was growing up. When I was little, my dad made it look seamless.

Work Together

When I think back to wonderful memories with my dad, the first thing that pops into my head is a picture of my dad and me at the gym, with his arms around me showing me the proper form of shooting a basketball. Sports were a huge part of my family's life and my childhood and my dad was always there, not just as a sideline watcher, but an active participant. He coached all my basketball teams from first grade into junior high, and my brother's baseball teams all the way from little league to all stars. It was something we could bond over and do together, forming inside jokes. In college, I learned that people tend to form a stronger connective bond when they work together toward a common goal, and though division champions for a YMCA basketball league might not be the noblest goal, I definitely felt like my dad and I were in it together, side-by-side every step of the way.

Be Interested

Even after I traded in free-throw practice for costume fittings, my dad's keen interest in what I was doing never changed. Though he really knew nothing about theatre, he always asked a million questions and wanted to know everything about what I was doing. Some might find this overbearing, but I never felt this way in the slightest, because my dad never asked any question to be nosy. I felt he was genuinely interested in the goings on of my life. I would tell him stories of funny things that happened, problems we were having with a certain scene, and the backstage drama that inevitably comes with high school theatre. My dad loved hearing about it, and would always ask follow-up questions about how my friends were doing, etc. He made my life and me feel interesting and exciting and worth sharing about, something every teenage girl needs. Some are so desperate for it they turn to unhealthy relationships, but I got it at home from my dad.

All through the growing up years, and especially now that I'm grown, I've loved hearing and seeing the ways in which I am just like my dad. We're both morning people and drive my mom crazy, we're both loud beyond belief, and many people have commented that our sense of humor is the same. Hearing this all my life was always so encouraging. I looked up to my dad, and if people were saying I was like him then I must be doing something right. I don't know if that's a "tip," per say, but honestly I think wanting to be like my dad (something most little kids want) and having people (or him) tell me I was made me feel encouraged.

Erin

My sister and I spent our childhood at the park, as "princesses" running away from the "giant." When we got sick, Daddy would pick us up from school. I used to jump into my dad's arms off of the top bunk. I would tell him to back up further and further. Then, I would leap off of the bed into the arms of my dad. I trusted him to catch me no matter how far away he was. We always called him "Dadman," since he was our superhero. He coached my soccer teams, read me stories, and made me laugh. He was invincible.

When I got into middle school, I still loved my dad. At that point, though, his superhero status started to fade. I started to see him as a person, instead. He still came to my soccer games and made me laugh.

He led my youth group, where all of my friends thought he was the best dad ever! Our relationship hit a turning point when the summer before I started high school. He took me on a six-hour road trip to Magic Mountain, just the two of us. At the beginning of the trip he told me that he knew that I was changing and becoming an adult, so he wanted to spend the trip getting to know the woman that I was becoming. We talked and laughed, as usual, but whenever we hit a lull in conversation, he asked me questions about myself. He asked about everything from my favorite movies and books to my hopes and dreams.

At the time, I thought it was cool and fun to go on a bunch of roller coasters and laugh with my dad. In retrospect, that week was when my daddy became my mentor and friend. He took the time and energy to prove to me that he cared about me, as a person. He had no expectations for me, except to share my life with him. That week he proved to me that I was valuable. From that point forward, I knew I was worth his time, his money, his energy and his love.

After that, I experienced high school and college, with the confidence that my daddy thought the world of me. One day, when I was in college, I called him to say hello. He answered the phone with a low voice. I asked what he was doing, and he replied that he was in a meeting. Apologizing for interrupting, I tried to get off the phone. He said to me, "Baby, it's okay. I just wanted to hear your little voice." This demonstrates my dad's constant availability to me, and his desire to connect with me. Now, I am 26 and getting married. My life has changed completely. I have a great job, an incredible fiancé, and wonderful friends. But I still know that whenever I call my daddy, he will drop everything just to hear my little voice.

Allison

Many things can and should contribute to a healthy and influential relationship, especially with regard to a father and his daughter. My father has done countless things to impact our relationship, ranging from taking me on special daddy-daughter dates to teaching me how to keep score in baseball, but there are three significant things he has done that have defined and impacted our relationship: he has pursued me, he has led me, and he has cherished me. These three things ultimately bestowed immeasurable worth in our relationship. His affections for me have been proven time and time again, and his relentless faithfulness to me as his precious daughter has made it impossible for me to mistake his love for anything but the outstanding, sacrificial love that it is.

Allison and Grant cooking up some dinner

1. He pursues me.

My father has made it known that he loves me through his fierce pursuit of my heart. The ways in which he pursued (and pursues, even still) me involved regularly planned daddy-daughter dates, selfless sacrifices, and countless phone calls to cover the tracks of long-distances apart. Most importantly, I believe that his pursuit of my heart began when I was a child and remained a faithful part of our daddy-daughter journey.

Though my father continues to woo me with quality time and known sacrifices, the daunting imposition of a long-distance relationship inflicted by my college years resulted in incessant phone calls from California to Arizona. I think I missed more calls than I ended up answering, mostly because my dad would call me almost any time he got into a car and had a second to talk. Instead of letting the endless miles drive a wedge in our relationship, he made an outstanding effort to stay as involved in my life as possible, making himself available at all hours of the day and night to talk, and faithfully pursuing me from hundreds of miles away.

2. He leads me.

As much as my father has acknowledged his need to protect me from the world, he has also recognized his role in preparing me for taking on the world as a young woman.

My dad has taught me many things: how to ride a bike, how to manage my money, how to serve others well, and how to preach the gospel boldly. It was his willingness to teach me how to do things, as opposed to simply doing things for me, that revealed to me how God has created me in a way that is meaningful and purposeful. Similar to the manner in which Jesus walked with his disciples, my dad has walked with me, allowing me to encounter God's intentions for my life while giving me the power to make decisions and experience freedom.

Through his willingness to lead me, he has taught me how to be a leader myself, and has taught me the value of responsibility and most importantly, of faithfulness to the Lord. He has steadily built a strong foundation of truth in my heart without silencing the voice that God has given me. Ultimately, he showed me how valuable I am as an individual child of God.

3. He cherishes me.

Above all else, my daddy cherishes me. He has pursued me since the day that I was born, and he has planted himself firmly into my life. He has led me throughout my life, teaching me valuable lessons and embracing me when I have chosen to blaze my own, disastrous path. And it is perhaps through these things that he has announced and claimed, shown and proven how much he truly, truly cherishes me.

It is ultimately the relationships in our lives that influence and shape who we become. My father has made it a priority to invest in my heart, mind and spirit consistently throughout my lifetime. His presence in my life has made a tremendous difference in who I am as a young woman. His daily decision to actively love me has inspired me to wholly embrace who God created me to be. My father's persistent pursuit of my heart has convinced me that I am more valuable than anything money could ever buy. It has been his fearless commitment to lead me that has encouraged me to believe that I am a capable woman of Christ who has the ability to accomplish anything that I might want to achieve. And, more than anything else, it has been my dad's ability to convey his endless love for me, his ability to communicate how much he truly values me that has enabled me to live in the ultimate freedom of Jesus Christ's love for me as his precious child. I am confident when I say that I would not be the woman I am today without the tireless, relentless, and faithful pursuits exhausted by my father.

Hannah

My dad is a dream-maker. He always encouraged us to dream big and to not limit our dreams based on finances or limitations others may put on us. He always says that God can do anything and I have learned that it is true because he helped me believe it. Dad always took interest in the things I cared about, whether it was softball, theater, swim team, singing, or travel. He always was interested, and he always showed up and cared. I have heard people say that you think of God like you think of your dad. If that is the case, then I think of God as one who cares for me, is always there for me, wants the best for me, and dreams big for me.

Dad was very intentional about taking trips with us. We have a tradition in our family that dad takes us on a trip when we turn 13 years old. My trip was to New York for five days. The goal of the trip is to spend time alone with my dad, and for him to talk about how a man should treat a woman. He took me to nice dinners, we went sightseeing, he opened doors for me, bought me flowers, took me to a Broadway show, and then walked me into Tiffany's and bought me a necklace! It was a trip I will never forget. It did make me realize that I want a guy in my life that treats me well and makes me feel special and not just by buying things for me or taking me to dinner but by treating me with respect.

Stu and Hannah in Uganda for their "18-year-old"
Father/Daughter trip

Then, my senior year we had the opportunity to go to London and Uganda. It was amazing. I had wanted to go to Africa since my dad went with my sister four years earlier. It had a big impact on my life. We saw tons of ministries in Uganda and it was life-changing. But it was also significant to do it with my dad. He made me feel special. It was deep, but we also laughed a lot. My dad is good at being deep but also funny. I like that about him.

I am thankful. I am thankful that he cares, that he is reliable, that he is funny, that he pushes me to dream big and not fear, and that he takes time to intentionally be with me.

Marisa

Daddy Daughter Dates:

I can still remember going to the bowling alley with my dad, and learning how to bowl and tabulate the scores on a grid with a golf pencil (before the cool TV monitors above every lane did it for you). There were also plenty of dinners out, and he took me to every Disney movie that came out. My dad even took me to get my ears pierced, which I still remember to this day. After the piercing, he took me to Miller's Outpost and bought me an outfit for the next day at school in honor of my new addition to my look (a green and white polka-dot matching short and shirt set).

Our Daddy Daughter dates continued through college (I went to a school close to his work at the time). I'd drive and pick him up from his office, and we would go to lunch.

Supportive:

My dad was at pretty much every soccer game. He didn't coach my teams, which I appreciated. He was there to support me, period. He was also at every choir concert, every theatre performance, and every volleyball match. He was present at the things that mattered to me.

Love Language:

My number one love language is words of affirmation. My dad was always affirming me with notes. Whether it was postcards from business trips (I still have them), or writing me a letter for each day I was away serving at camp on work crew (I still have all of them, too), my dad encouraged me in the way that was most valuable to me. He is still intentional now, with texting and emailing.

The effect:

My dad set a high standard of what I looked for in men—not just in a romantic sense, but in how I viewed men in general. His integrity and morality (which played out in how he treated my family and me) set the bar for what I expected from men, especially men in leadership positions (future bosses, future co-workers, friends, etc.). Also, when I made the decision to follow Jesus, the love I had experienced by my earthly father made a huge difference. I knew what it felt like to be loved and cherished as a daughter, and that directly correlated for me to my relationship with God the Father. Lastly, the support and love I received from my dad has given me confidence in myself to pursue the things that I love and feel I was made for here on earth.

Kristy

So much of who I am today is because of my dad. I grew up knowing I am loved, believing I am capable of big things and supported for what I choose to do in all aspects of my life. My dad is firm yet forgiving, busy yet available, frugal yet generous, serious yet silly, and other qualities I now find myself trying to replicate in my own life and model for my own kids.

I think one of the most meaningful things that my dad did while I was growing up was give me responsibility and trust me to do things on my own. He taught me the value of hard work and he gave me big tasks that showed me how to be responsible. He supervised but not micromanaged me, and I knew that he believed in me. I knew that he thought I could do it, and many times that was enough for me.

I also appreciated that I was always given the opportunity to learn how to do things that sometimes young girls don't get the opportunity to learn. He taught me to check the oil in my car, change a tire when I had a flat, drive a boat, tow a trailer, play football, put on snow chains, build a deck, put up Christmas lights, and work in the yard. Although I knew I was "Daddy's little girl," I also was taught to be confident and capable of doing things on my own.

Those have been great life lessons for me and I have had to call upon that knowledge many times. More than just calling upon that knowledge, it has instilled in me a sense of confidence which the Lord has used in my life to lead others, to speak in front of groups, to speak my mind, to feel comfortable running events and trips and in my work where I am surrounded mostly by men.

I am also thankful for the importance he placed on faith and family, because that has become the cornerstone of my life. As my own father taught me lessons, protected, cared for, served, corrected, and guided me, I learned to listen to, respect, admire, and love my heavenly Father. For that I am most grateful.

Carly

Not too long ago, I did something irresponsible with my car. I think the brakes had been going out, and I had driven it way too long in that condition. My dad was not happy. One afternoon, I somehow got my car over to my parents' house, right before the brakes completely went out, and I remember my dad saying, "I have 35 minutes to try and fix this before I have to go." Long story short, he came in about 40 minutes later saying, "I don't know what to do, I can't figure it out. I think it's going to cost you a lot of money."

Immediately I started to cry, and said, "What am I going to do? I don't have that amount of money!" He said, "Well what would you do if I weren't here?" and he stormed off in frustration. I began to cry while my mom consoled me, telling me he didn't mean it and so on, and I said, "No, he's right. What would I do?" A few minutes later, as my dad was getting ready to leave for the retreat, he came upstairs, gave me a big hug and said, "Carly, I'm your daddy, and I will always take care of you. It's my job."

I use that story as an example because dads aren't perfect. My dad has a temper sometimes and gets frustrated with me sometimes, but he is the first person I call when I stumble upon trouble or worry. He always tells me that everything's going to be okay, no matter the situation.

My dad was the one who not only told me about Jesus, but he modeled what his love looked like growing up. No matter the situation, good or bad, he would share Jesus with us kids. The way he loves my mom is what Christ's love looks like to me. I'm only half-joking when I say that I'm still single because I'm waiting for that kind of love that lasts a lifetime, honoring Christ.

Most of all, my dad has shown me grace. I was a tough, rebellious kid and I liked to do things my own way. My parents never enabled me, but there were times when I really learned the hard way and they were there to hold me and comfort me in times of trouble. I love reflecting on the greatness of my father, who is who he is, because of God our Father!

Bree

My dad was super strict and a perfectionist, but he pursued me hard in high school and I am grateful for it now.

"Strict," Perfectionist, Confident

I have a great dad! We made it through the inevitably difficult teenage years. I wanted freedom, and he was pulling back the reins. I am grateful he did. At the time, a very strict father and an independent daughter combined to create animosity and a little resentment in our home. Although I did not admit it at the time, I was a little grateful for this as it gave me an excuse to not get into trouble and it always gave me an out since all my friends knew my dad was strict. I knew what the rules were and if I did not follow them I knew the consequences. I respected this and I respected my father for not being wishy-washy.

His word was his word. He was a perfectionist and this pushed me to try to succeed in all that I did. He was never disappointed in me—just questioned or encouraged me to work hard. Although he was strict and a perfectionist, he built up confidence in me in the right ways. He never spoke poorly of me and was never degrading. I worked hard and did not complain about it. I am grateful for this confidence and work ethic he instilled in me.

Presence

My dad was always present in my life, even though my parents were divorced. He was at every game and everything at school, and we always sat down for dinner together at the table. I stayed with my dad on Wednesdays and every other weekend, yet somehow I saw him many more times than that throughout the week. He was my dad, and he did not let their divorce get in the way of raising his kids and spending time with them.

Our relationship did a 180 the second I went to college, meaning the animosity and resentment of his strictness went away. Although I'm sure he did this at home, I noticed it more when I went away. He pursued me and encouraged me personally, not just for my sporting events or school activities. He called me nearly every day just to say hi. He came to visit. By my dad calling nearly every day, he knew what was going on in my life. When hard situations came up, I did not have to worry about making up stories, or worry about how he would react. I could be honest and open because we had developed a great friendship.

Our friendship continues on today, and so do our great phone calls checking in. Although my dad and I have different stances on faith, he has a great respect for what I do. Because of daily conversations, he knew my role in ministry was the best fit for me. He changed from being a strict perfectionist on what he thought my career path should be, to encouraging me to pursue a career in ministry. I am so grateful for my dad!

Molly

The sweetest and fondest memories I have with my father are the times that I was alone with him. My dad made a point from the beginning of his parenthood to spend time with each of his children individually, which strongly influenced each of our relationships with him. I can remember getting so excited to have date nights with dad. My mom would curl my hair, I would put on a fancy dress, and he would take me out to dinner, alone.

I specifically remember one night we went on a date when I was about seven. After dinner, he took me to buy magnetic earrings, something that I was dying to have. Instead of getting the magnetic earrings, he told me I could get my ears pierced. For the next several weeks I proudly flashed everyone the cubic zirconia in my little ears. "Look what my dad let me do!"

These date nights were undoubtedly fun and spontaneous, but the mere fact that they created time alone for us to talk is what I believe built the foundation of our strong father-daughter relationship.

When I got a little older, my dad started taking me on trips to New York. I felt so special and important because it was only going to be Dad and me for a few days. It was over dinner and sightseeing that we could talk about things, like where I wanted to go to college and what I wanted to do when I grew up. These conversations, which ultimately resulted in deep trust and friendship, were ones that were hard to have in the chaos of day-to-day life at home. To this day, I am still so thankful for my time alone with my dad. He has become my solid rock and our talks bring me a sense of safety and relief.

Jim and Molly enjoying a cruise

His unconditional love for my mother, his ability to teach me important lessons in philanthropy and faith through his own actions, and his "don't sweat the small stuff" attitude have all been important factors in raising me to be the woman I am today.

Carlie

Wow, when I sit down thinking about what to write, I have so many thoughts. I don't think I can sum up in only a few paragraphs how well I was raised! But here are a few things that come to mind:

Looking back on when I was younger and even today, I think such a huge thing to me is how loving my dad is and how much he shows it all the time. When I was a teenager or even younger and made a mistake, or if I did something I wasn't supposed to do, it didn't matter what it was, I was still shown unconditional love. Even when there were certain things I did that I was ashamed and embarrassed about, knowing that my dad still loved me (because he was so great at expressing that) just made me feel so much better, and I knew that things would get better. It didn't matter if I was being rude and disrespectful. He still showed how much he loved me. My dad never turned his back on a situation or just brushed it under the rug. He wanted to work through the issue at hand. That in itself showed me how much he loved me. He taught me to work through the problem instead of ignoring it, even though that is not my area of expertise. No matter the situation, he is always great at expressing his love.

Carlie and Mike on their big day

My dad always set such a great example as a husband. All my years growing up, the way he loved my mom and respected her was something I looked up to. And I knew that he was the kind of husband I wanted. He taught me right from wrong. He set such a great example to me in how he involved God in his everyday life, and he instilled that in us. He always encouraged me to do my best. He was (and is) always so supportive. There were lots of little things he did that made an impact as well. My dad took us girls to get our nails done twice a month, and I always looked forward to that. I received a single rose on Valentine's Day, even when I was in high school. It was such a good feeling at that age (the awkward teenage years) to know that no matter what, your dad loves you.

There are a million and one things I could say that my dad did to help me grow and be who I am today. My dad and mom have both been such great role models to have as parents and as a married couple. I love having them to look up to! I hope these thoughts help more fathers be just like my dad to their daughters, because I know I'm pretty lucky to have the dad that I have!

Cindy

My dad is a great dad for many reasons, but I'd say the one trait that carries through everything is consistency. He has been a faithful spouse to my mom, and honored his commitments to her. He has been a consistent father to his children. He always, always followed through on his word. If he said he would be at a sporting event, he was there. If he said he'd take us to dinner, he would. If he said he'd discipline us a certain way, he would.

Oddly enough, I think following through on discipline is the part I'm most thankful for. He didn't give empty threats, and he showed us he really believed in the values and character traits he was teaching us in the home.

Finally, he has always been consistent in his walk with the Lord. He faithfully honors God with his life, time, money, and heart. His choice to day in and day out be this kind of father is what has allowed me to know that I can count on him through and through. He made a commitment to be a faithful person, committed to his responsibilities, no matter the cost or what he felt like, and then stuck to it for a lifetime.

My dad's consistent love and commitment to God and our family grew a solid sense of self-worth in me. I don't doubt that I'm valuable or worthy of love. My experience in working with teens and young adults has taught me that this is rare. I'm extremely lucky to have my sense of value intact. Believing I am worth something has played out in nearly every relationship. It gives me a hopeful disposition for the future, and helps me forgive others and myself. Knowing my value has allowed me to make decisions for myself, apart from what others think or say about me. I have bad days and lose my way at times, but deep down, my dad's faithful love reminds me that I'm a precious daughter of the King.

Rachel

Where to start? My earliest memories are of my dad coming in each night, jumping high like Superman and landing on us in the bed my sister and shared, to say good night. We would laugh, and he would get in trouble from my mom. It became our little nightly joke and Mom would play along, too. But then he would settle us down and pray, "Now I lay me down to sleep . . . ." He would try to pray about other stuff, too, but we always made him pray that prayer before he could leave.

Also very impactful was all the time he spent playing with us. He could have sat on the couch, gone to the gym, read a book, or any number of things. He chose to play with us. We played everything . . . . cards, board games, football (yes, we can all run patterns), baseball, basketball, just about anything.

As I look back I am thankful for a dad who placed his faith in Jesus Christ and expected the best of me. Thanks, Dad!

Shauna

As long as I can remember, even the smallest thing my dad did for me made me feel so special and loved—whether it was cuddling on the couch or taking me to get my nails painted while he got a haircut. My dad was always so good at letting me help him fix something that was broken, or teaching me how to build a playhouse, and it made me feel independent.

As the years went by and life brought on new challenges, I always felt safe coming to him for just about anything. He was so good about thinking over every situation before he gave me an answer. Friends changed, but he always welcomed any of them. Picking up my friends and me for "off campus" lunch in junior high was such a special thing, because none of their dads would do that. Our home was always open for friends to hang out, and that in return made us want to be there.

Once I became a teenager and almost impossible to parent, he kept such a calm attitude and approach to any situation. I can only pray to be that way with my kids. I don't know how he managed to do it, but whenever I needed a punishment, he seemed to turn it into making me a better person. The thing that always bettered me was that he related most talks to mistakes he made as a child, and really showed how he only wants the best for me in life.

Now that I am a parent myself, I still look to my dad for those "positive" talks. I love how he can relate life's issues to how God would want me to be or react in any given situation. My dad molded me into the strong, independent woman I am today!

Stephanie

My dad was a man of few words but big actions. A quiet man who never verbally taught life lessons, but instead spoke with acts of humility, generosity, hard work, and kindness. All I had to do was observe and emulate. He silently demanded respect and obedience. I never wanted to disappoint him. He joked and teased, and created a home environment filled with unwavering love and laughter—lots of laughter. His outlook on life is just like him, simple yet profound: "Love God and love people. That's it." It's what I now strive for every day.

From Alan:

Wow, what a group of testimonies! Wouldn't every dad hope their daughters would say those things about them? Here's what I heard:

My dad is invested and verbal about his love for my mom and me.

My dad disciplines me.
My dad tells me I am amazing, and I believe him.
My dad's unconditional love makes me confident in who I am.
My dad is spontaneous.
My dad makes me laugh.
My dad and I have inside jokes.
My dad asks a lot of questions.
My dad is present and encouraging.

My dad loves the Lord, his wife, and his daughters, and I see it.

My dad pushes me to be the best I can be.

My dad's involvement in my life has had a huge impact on how I view relationships and dating.

My dad is honest.

My dad actively pursues a loving relationship with my mom.

My dad's love gives me security and confidence.

My dad embarrasses me around guys and I appreciate it.

My dad and I have adventures.

My dad is fun.

My dad shows up when it is painful.

My dad teases me.

My dad challenges me.

My dad is my valentine.

My dad loves his family and loves Jesus.

My dad adopts our friends as family.

My dad gives his time to the church, and is more generous than anyone I know.

My dad takes me on dates and pursues me.

My dad sets aside intentional time to spend with me.

My dad makes me feel like I am more important than his work.

My dad leads me and teaches me.

My dad cherishes me.

My dad encourages me to dream big.

My dad is supportive.

My dad set a high standard of what I looked for in men.

My dad gave me a good picture of my heavenly Father.

My dad made me believe I am capable of big things.

My dad gives me responsibility and trusts me to do things on my own.

My dad believes in me.

My dad gives me the opportunity to learn things that girls don't always get to learn.

My dad not only told me about Jesus, he also modeled what His love looked like.

My dad pushed me to be the best I could be.

My dad takes me on trips.

My dad initiates conversations, which ultimately results in deep trust and friendship.

My dad always set such a great example as a husband.

My dad is consistent.

My dad faithfully honors God with his life, time, money, and heart.

My dad is proud of me.

My dad has time for me.

My dad has a calm attitude and approach to any situation.

My dad loves God and loves people.

Men, that's a pretty good list! Those words are not mine. They come straight from the mouths of daughters who were loved well by their dads. Take this list and live it out. Infuse these principles into the way you live and love your daughter. We have taken the mystery out of raising your daughter. These great girls who turned out well have spoken. Now, go do these things!

Real Talk

"My dad has made it remarkably obvious that there is nothing I could do that would change how much he loves me. He has cherished me since day one of my little baby life, he has told me over and over again how much he loves me, and he has shown me through his countless sacrifices, phone calls, and investments in my life that I am the most precious thing to him.

Each step of our relationship has reminded me of his persistent and unconditional love for me: a love that allows me to further understand how much Christ loves me. It is this reflection of my Heavenly Father's love that convinces me of how incredibly significant my earthly father is in my life."

Chapter 8

Daddy's Girl:
Brittany Smyth's Story

"What are you?"

"Prized Possession!"

"And . . ."

"Don't you forget it!"

When I consider the woman I am today, I realize that this small conversation played an integral part in shaping me into the person I am right now. These four lines represent a life-long conversation that has taken place between my dad and me. I never realized how powerful these words were or how lucky I was to hear them on a regular basis. My dad began this conversation before I could speak in complete sentences or comprehend what meaning it carried. These words were some of the first words added to my lexicon. To this day, there is only one answer when my dad asks the simple question, "What are you?" Without any hesitation I reply, "Prized possession." "And . . ." "Don't you forget it!" It's second nature. It's who I am. It's who I will always be.

It's only been over the last couple years that I've realized just how powerful the words "prized possession" are. Today I'm an independent, 25-year-old woman, and I realize I would not be who I am without the unconditional love of my dad. I've taken the last few months to really reflect on what it means to be Alan Smyth's daughter, and how those two little words have impacted my life. I am overwhelmed to say the least. Overwhelmed with how incredibly lucky I am and how much I've been blessed by my dad.

As I dissect the words, "Prized Possession," I realize it's not the words themselves that are so powerful. It's the actions behind them—the actions my dad took to make sure that they were not just empty syllables. Without action, there is no meaning, and my dad has made it his life's mission to show me this. Because of this, there is no question in my mind that my dad loves me, and I know beyond a shadow of a doubt that he would go to the ends of the earth for me.

Alan and Brittany hanging out in LA

I think it's safe to say that I am a Daddy's Girl. When I look back on my childhood, I can see why. Some of my fondest memories are with my dad. From coaching my soccer teams to taking me on father-daughter getaways, to spending summers at Young Life camp watching him speak to hundreds of campers about the love Jesus has for us, he has been my biggest role model.

One of the biggest highlights has to be the father-daughter getaways. Every summer from the time I was five years old until I graduated from high school, he made it a priority to spend one-on-one time with me. No distractions—just him and me.

Our first getaway was to Disneyland, and I remember it like it was yesterday. Driving from the Bay Area down to the Magic Kingdom, listening to Disney soundtracks the whole way. This trip laid the foundation for many more trips to come. In the years following, Dad took me on so many adventures and gave me the opportunity to check things off my life list. My dreams were his dreams and he was determined to give me some of the most amazing experiences. Anything from horseback riding, to mall-hopping and shopping extravaganzas, to swimming with the dolphins in Hawaii, he made it all happen.

If you know my dad, you can probably guess that horseback riding or shopping all day at the mall is not exactly on the top of his priority list, but I was, and being the amazing dad that he is, he took me on one adventure after the other and made life long memories with me. While we had some really cool experiences together, I now understand that it was not so much what we did that had value, but it was the fact that we did them together. In hindsight, all this time that he invested in me was building me up to become a confident, independent woman.

As I continue to take this walk down memory lane, I realize the biggest gift he ever gave me was being present in my life. He was always there to cheer me on and tell me how proud he was of me. From elementary school, chaperoning field trips and coaching soccer teams, to junior high and high school being at every volleyball game. From late-night dessert runs after my mom went to bed, to busting me out of school for father-daughter lunch dates. When I turned 21 on May 18, he took me for my first official drink at 12:01 the night of May 17. I was so proud to be carded, only to show my license that revealed I'd been 21 for two minutes! The server said, "Well, Happy Birthday!" and with a big smile, I said, "Thank you."

We even recently took a trip to Las Vegas together, to see a show and have fun. I was surprised when we walked down to the front row, dead center, to find our seats. My dad was surprised when they pulled him up on stage to dance with a clown in front of a packed house. I think it's pretty clear that he made his relationship with me one of his highest priorities.

While my dad has done many hands-on, intentional things to be the best dad he could be to me, I have also been impacted indirectly by the way he lives his daily life. It has not only been the extravagant trips or crazy spur of the moment outings, but it's the everyday life stuff that played a huge role in shaping who I am and want to be. It's what he chooses to do in the midst of crazy chaos or just in the quiet moments at home when no one is around.

One thing in particular that stands out in my mind is how he has loved my mom so well. He has given me an amazing example of how a real man should treat a woman. I've been able to witness firsthand what a healthy, successful marriage looks like. After 25 years of watching my dad interact with my mom, I know for sure that he has every quality that I want to find in my future husband. It is because of the amazing example that he has set that I know what I deserve, and I will not settle for anything less. For that, I am extremely grateful.

When I put this all together and think about what it all means, I realize that I owe a huge thank you to my dad. It is because of him that I am a confident, strong, independent woman. I have never felt the need to search for love and acceptance in other places. In many ways, it's this love that my dad has shown me that has saved me from many "worldly escapes." I've never had the desire to find comfort or my identity in drugs, alcohol or boys. It wasn't until hearing the tragic stories of many girls who don't have a dad in the picture that I realized how rare this is. I've heard story after story of beautiful, amazing girls who have felt like they had to find love in all the wrong places. The idea of not having a present dad absolutely breaks my heart, and I am forever grateful for all the time and energy my dad has invested in me.

As I move forward, and continue to explore everything this crazy world has to offer, I will do so with confidence. Confidence in where I came from, who I am, and who I am becoming. It is the kind of confidence that runs deep. The kind that is fostered over a long period of time as a result of the unconditional love from a father.

So, in conclusion, "Thank you, Dad." You have impacted my life in a way that words cannot explain. You mean more to me than you'll ever know.

I love you,

Your "Prized Possession"

Real Talk

"My Dad has never failed to tell me that he believes in me, that he is proud of me, and that he will continue to remain steadfast in his love for me. My father's unfailing faith in my character and his investment in my relationship with Christ have combined to prepare me well for the many worldly life experiences that, inevitably, attempt to influence me."

Chapter 9

Conclusion

This project has been an incredible experience for me. Never really knowing where my research was going or exactly what I would find out, I have had a total blast digging into this content. The project really started 25 years ago, when I was blessed with a daughter. Born male into a family with only brothers, I never saw how a daughter was supposed to be raised. I made it up as I went along, hoping I did some things right, but I'm sure I made some mistakes as well. I am very proud of my Brittany and the woman she has become. She has made great choices along the way, and while I'd like to think I had a little something to do with it, I certainly don't claim all the credit. Not even close. Brittany had a great mom pouring into her as well. And, so much of parenting is out of our control. Many great guys do all the right things, and their daughters still struggle. Parenting is not a formula, and it cannot be totally predicted. It's more art than science.

However, I do believe in the scientific laws of nature. We reap what we sow. If we invest consistently in our daughters and offer them unconditional love, we are more likely to reap satisfying rewards along the way.

As I conclude, I'd like to summarize my journey and my findings for you in three categories: The Big Three, Redemption, and Going Forward.

THE BIG THREE

So what did I learn in this process? What bubbled up as most significant? How can you be a better dad? Most guys I know just want the answer—"Just tell me what to do!"—but it's kind of tough to reduce such a huge topic down to bullet points. The reality of raising a daughter is so complex that it cannot be put into a list. There are so many case-by-case scenarios and so many different DNA strands in fathers and daughters, that it is really hard to make a definitive statement on parenting.

However, three main concepts seemed to come up more than any others. The majority of girls I interviewed all said, in their own words, that these three concepts were most significant in their lives. Many dads I interviewed said they intentionally attempted to accomplish these three concepts more than any others, too. So, if both the daughters and fathers alike said these three elements are most important to a healthy relationship, then I guess we'd better pay attention!

The First Concept

The first significant impact that was communicated to me was the importance of daughters seeing their dads faithfully love their wives. It made a huge impact when daughters saw their parents modeling a healthy marriage. Dads being affectionate, loving, honoring and respectful of their wives communicated a sense of security and painted a clear picture of who God is. Additionally, a dad actively loving his wife gave a great example of the kind of guy that the daughter would be looking for. This one concept will affect multiple generations, because your daughter will make a better choice in a husband if you do a great job at loving your wife. This will not only affect your daughter's adult life, but the kind of grandchildren you have, as well. This is a big outcome that you might not necessarily think of, because it does not directly involve your daughter.

Love and serve your wife!

The Second Concept

The second element of the Big Three that made a huge impact on girls was when their dads lived out an authentic faith. Not coincidentally, the dads I talked to all worked hard at this and thought this was important, too. A dad living out an authentic faith where God is honored in the home makes a huge impact on the kids, specifically on our girls. A genuine faith lived out is marked by grace, honesty, forgiveness, unconditional love, hard work, and wisdom, among many other traits. Obviously, these things lived out in a family would make a huge impact. A daughter would be loved, encouraged and lifted up in a home like this. Any daughter growing up in a home like this has a better chance of thriving through adolescence. Dads said faith was a main priority of their parenting, and daughters said this was huge for them. This is also big because we see over and over that adolescent girls with a distant relationship with their earthly fathers struggle to conceive of a heavenly Father. There is a correlation between your faith and your daughter's ability to have a faith. That correlation will make a huge difference in her life path.

Love and serve your God!

The Third Concept

The third part of the Big Three: a father spending intentional time with his daughter. This can be broken down into two categories. First, there is the ongoing time spent during a day, week, or month. Maybe this means going to one of their games, or maybe it looks like a lunch date. In any case, a dad showing up and intentionally making time for his daughter makes a huge impact. There is no replacing plain old time spent together. It matters far less what you are doing, and matters far more that you are simply doing something together. That you are present in her life! This provides opportunity for surface level conversations, which pave the way for deeper, more meaningful conversations. Time spent with your daughter is paramount, because it gives you credibility to have the harder conversations later on.

In addition to time spent during the week, another category of time came in the form of taking trips together. Many dads told stories of the trips they took with their daughters. More than one daughter called them "adventures." What better way to build memories than to have adventures with someone? After all, "It's only an adventure if you are not sure you are going to make it." Who better to have "adventures" with than your daughter, with whom you are hoping to bond? There were many dads who actually took their daughters on trips, and these daughters spoke glowingly about them.

I went into great detail on some of these in Chapter 6. Trips to Hawaii, Africa, NYC, Disneyland, and everywhere in between made an impact. Trips provide the rare combination of fun, adventure, uncertainty, and new experiences. What better way to spend a few days each year than to plan a trip with your daughter! Many of the dads I spoke with did this very intentionally, and daughters I spoke with were greatly impacted when this happened. You can buy "stuff," but you really can't buy memories and adventure!

Love and serve your daughter by spending time with her!

There they are! Those are the Big Three that bubbled up from this project. While there are hundreds of nuances with everything you might do, if a dad focuses intentional effort on these three items, his daughter will be much better off because of it. These three elements have been tested, proven and communicated to me over and over again. Go for it!

REDEMPTION

The great thing about focusing one's life on who God is and what He wants to do in your life is that He makes all things new. 2 Corinthians 5:17 says, "If anyone is in Christ, he is a new creation. The old is gone, the new has come." This is great news for all of us on so many levels. Isn't it great that God's grace is big enough to cover a multitude of sins, mistakes, goof ups and miscues? This is great news for our personal lives, because it means that we don't have to live with our old mistakes and old ways of thinking. We can become shiny and new and have a new life through Christ.

Now, apply this to parenting, and the news just got even better. While I interviewed lots of dads for this book and heard lots of great strategies and philosophies, most were quick to say that they made plenty of mistakes. All were humble enough, or perhaps wise enough, to know that they were far from perfect. Isn't it great that God's grace is big enough to cover our parenting blunders and shortcomings?

There is redemption for us all. In Chapter 1, I told you about my dear friend who wished to remain anonymous simply to protect her mother. She told of a painful experience with her father who "cursed" her when she was five years old. She said her entire life trajectory was altered because of that experience.

At the end of her father's life, my friend also tells how she sat at her dad's deathbed and held his hand. She shares how her dad gazed into her eyes and called her his "angel." What an enormous chasm they had crossed over the lifetime of hurt she experienced. But what a joy to know that God had repaired their relationship enough for it to end in this manner. I can only imagine the redemption her father felt, knowing that the little girl he had cursed and pushed away so long ago was comforting him on his deathbed.

When I asked my friend how this reconciliation happened, this was her reply:

> The day I met Jesus, at 12 years old, I walked in
> my house and looked at my mom and dad, and felt this
> overwhelming sense of forgiveness for them. It was
> automatic and, now, looking back, I realize that was the

Holy Spirit in me. So, in one sense, the forgiveness was instant, but in another sense, forgiving was a life-long process that involved revisiting painful memories and experiencing the presence of Jesus in those memories. It was a life-long process of getting to know my Heavenly Father, and letting him become the Father I never knew as a child. That process involved therapy and counseling at different points; a lot of love and grace from the family of God; a lot of time in reflective prayer; letting my heavenly Father love me; the love and kindness of a good husband; and the gift of watching my husband love our little girl like little girls were meant to be loved. Watching my husband love our daughter was one of the significant tools God used to heal my own brokenness involving my dad.

I think it's important for dads to know that the heavenly Father is going to graciously take up the slack of their failures as fathers. God is going to use their failures as opportunities to reveal himself as the heavenly Father we all long for. Even the best father here is a faint shadow of our real Father in heaven. And that's okay. Dads, your daughter's wellbeing does not ultimately rest on your shoulders. It rests on the much bigger shoulders of the One to whom we all belong.

Additionally in Chapter 1, I quoted another anonymous friend. I referred to her as "one of my favorite people in the world." She was sent down a dangerous and painful path of life due to her father's actions. All of this hurt, pain and dysfunction can be traced back to an absent, dysfunctional father. Her tragic childhood and painful life path resulted in painful ramifications. Now, as this friend shares her story, she joyfully speaks of how the Lord rescued her and holds her life together. Thankfully, she has survived her circumstances, and with a tear in her eye, she says that the Lord saved her in every way. God brought her a great husband and they have fantastic kids out flourishing in the world. She once told me that she would be a "statistic," had the Lord not intervened and redeemed her life. I can't say that her relationship with her dad was repaired, but she speaks strongly of God's redemption in her own life. She will give Jesus credit for rescuing her from her life's circumstances.

For You, Too

There is redemption for you, too! You may have already messed up big time. You may have already missed out on so much. However, it is never too late! When this project first started, an old friend of mine said, "Where was this seven years ago when I needed it?" I told him, "Get started now—It's not too late." It may be true that you were formerly unarmed for the task, but now that you have read this book, you have philosophy, strategy and testimonies for how to move forward. Additionally, we've designed a website—www.myfatherdaughter.com—as a place for conversation and resources as you move forward. From the website, you can subscribe to our blog and receive regular nuggets of thought to help you in your journey. You are no longer alone. But, it starts with YOU. You have to resolve that it is vitally important to love your daughter in the way she is designed and deserves to be loved. There is redemption waiting for you with your daughter. She wants to forgive you and she wants to be right with you. Lean into the redemption God has for you. Start today!

Going Forward

As you move forward, you are in one of four groups.

Your daughter is 0-5 years old
Your daughter is 6-12 years old
Your daughter is 13-18 years old
Your daughter is over 18

Each age group has significantly different issues and complexities. I am not intending to impersonate a child psychologist here. You can easily find clinical advice, if you are interested. But let me give you a little lay advice from an experienced dad who has somehow made his way through each stage. Here are a few things that I remember, and a few things for you to consider in each stage of your daughter's life.

Stage 1: 0-5 Years

When Brittany was 0-5, I was a brand new dad. Everything was new and exciting. Things that marked this stage were merry-go-round rides, Easy Bake ovens, pictures with Santa, pogs, and poopy diapers. I coached (and attended) my first soccer game when Brittany played on the "Kittens." She learned so much about teamwork, hard work and self-confidence while playing for the Kittens. I experienced my "Grand Slam of Input" during these years, and that greatly affected how I would parent from then on. We had our first Father/Daughter

Getaway to Disneyland when she was five, and the trajectory was on its way.

If you are in this stage with your daughter, let me encourage you to soak up every minute. It will never be as easy to spend intentional time with your daughter than it is right now, when she has nothing else to do. And, she is preprogrammed to think you are great. You are not yet operating out of a "cool" deficit and she is your biggest fan. Use this time to set up your tradition of Father/Daughter Getaways. Take your first trip with your daughter. Do something super fun and relatively extravagant. (Keep in mind, "extravagant" for a four or five year-old will be different than for a 16 year-old. Pace yourself!) Set the stage for the next 15 years. While there won't be a ton of deep conversation, she is watching you, and learning lessons of faith, love, and marriage. Those things are being imprinted on her little heart, mind, and soul. It can be any way you want it to be. She is very available and very open to any idea you have. You are a superhero to her. Roll with it! Have fun! Take advantage of these years.

Stage 2: 6-12 Years

These are the elementary school years. This time in our lives was marked by breakfasts at McDonalds before school, "Lunch and a Trinket" when I broke her out of school, more soccer teams, braces, becoming a big sister, and attending lots of field trips. During these years, we solidified the Father/Daughter Getaways and saw lots of Disney movies.

Near the end of stage two, your daughter could begin testing the rules and pushing the limits. She is becoming a young woman and the outside influences are starting to rise up. Make sure you are speaking words of authentic beauty and of your unconditional love for her during these years. Be redundant. Repeat yourself a lot. Let there be no doubt in your daughter's mind that she is absolutely cherished by her dad. Later in Stage 2, your daughter may bring up the topic of wearing make-up and dressing more maturely. In part, this will happen because other families will likely be less conservative than yours. Decide what your standards will be before she starts asking. Make it seem like this is the way it is. If she senses you are making it up as you go along, she will sense weakness, and pounce.

Stage 3: 13-18 Years

Look out! Junior high and high school are here. Things that marked these years for us were volleyball, long Saturday tournaments, school dances, stressful acne outbreaks, a move from Northern California to Southern Cal, learning to drive, and a Father/Daughter Getaway to Hawaii. Now begins the payoff for all of your intentional effort during Stage 1 and Stage 2. It's a good thing you have been building into your daughter, because you will need all the positive relationship you can get.

You might catch her in a lie and have to confront her (or worse). You will become skeptical of boys who are starting to hang around. You will become over-protective. She will get in the car of another kid driving, and you will be nervous until she walks through the door at the end of the night. You think you lost sleep in Stage 1? You will not sleep well in this stage either.

Make sure you have a dating and dressing policy by the beginning of Stage 3. Do not let that one just happen. Take the lead and start talking about it at the end of Stage 2. Then, it won't be a surprise when you actually need it. It will already be in place. Your thoughtful policy will likely be different than most of her friends and everything she is seeing advertised. Prepare for a battle.

In our case, we didn't let Brittany wear spaghetti strap tops when she was little. She never understood why and would get mad at us now and then. We told her that it really didn't matter now (when she was 9 or 10) but that it would matter later when she was older. Then, when she started to become a "woman" and I wanted her to dress modestly, the policy was already in place and I wasn't making something up as a reaction.

In the case of dating, the policy was set in place long before her first date: I had to meet the boy before the actual date happened. In other words, I couldn't be meeting the kid the same time he was picking her up. He had to come over and sit on the couch with me and enter into some conversation prior to date night. It wasn't my intention to scare the kid, but I needed him to understand that I was involved in Brittany's life and how valuable she was to me. His intimidation was simply a bonus. Really, I just wanted to meet the boy before date night so I had a feeling of what we were up against. Of course I got some static on this one, but I potentially had no idea who this kid was and what kind of upbringing he experienced.

Whatever little bit of accountability he gleaned from meeting me was imperative.

I also bought Brittany a little martial arts weapon called a Kubaton, which is perfect for gouging out eyes or anything else, if needed. She kept one in her car at all times. I taught her a few self-defense moves, and told her about the three main target zones on a male—the eyes, throat, and groin—and I gave her a few pointers guaranteed to temporarily disable any unwanted advance. I let her know that should she ever actually need to repel a male, these moves would be sure to give her some much needed space. I said, too, that she'd have to fully commit to the move or it wouldn't work, and I gave her my permission to disable anyone who she deemed an unwanted aggressor.

When you are teaching your 17-year-old daughter how to disable a male through a series of rapid shots to the groin, you may wonder, "Whatever happened to swing sets and Easy Bake Ovens?" I know I did. Time flies, Dad, so don't waste it.

Stage 3 is a critical time in your daughter's life. These are tumultuous years fraught with many landmines. She will need you to stay close, even if she says otherwise. Be involved, and stay engaged. Be near. The world is going to make some serious withdrawals during these years, so make sure you have made plenty of deposits!

Stage 4: Over 18 Years

Whew! You made it! While you will always be your daughter's parent, things have definitely changed by now. She is now more of a friend, and you will love having adult conversations with her. Things that marked this time period for us were going away to college, a semester in Africa; tattoo on/tattoo off; me running off an unwanted boy (unwanted by me, not her); moving back home from college and her getting an adult job; and moving into her own apartment. When Brittany was in college, I gave her money for her roommate and her to see the movie *Taken*. She was talking about going on a spring break trip to NYC, and I needed her to see that movie first. She was still a bit naive to the big world out there (my opinion, not hers), and I wanted to heighten her awareness toward the scumbag predators that exist out there. While I'm sure that movie has taken some Hollywood liberties in making a fun movie, I know that the essence of the movie is true. I know there are bad guys out there, looking for young females to prey upon. I needed her to see it and create awareness of the scumbags who wanted to do her harm.

Wow. It seems like only yesterday I was at Happy Hollow, feeding the goats and playing in the "crooked house" with her. Now my little girl is gone. "Gone," meaning that, by the world's standards, she is no longer "little." And, she no longer lives under my roof. However, she will most assuredly always remain my little girl and my "Prized Possession." She is a young woman, and she is happy, healthy, confident and independent. The resolution that I adopted in 1991 served us well. I resolved to intentionally love her and stay close to her. I resolved to give her all the tools she needed to grow up happy and healthy while making life giving choices. I was resolute that if she were to make poor choices later in her life, they would be on her and not on me. I was determined that she could never say that her dad was not involved in her life. No one is claiming perfection here, but I can rest in knowing that my daughter turned out great and is headed on the right trajectory. I have had a blast being Brittany's dad for the last 25 years and I can't wait for the next 25. She has been launched in a certain direction, and I can't wait to see how God further blesses her journey.

May God richly bless you and your efforts in the sacred task of raising your daughter. The fact that you have read this book tells me you are further down the path than most dads. You can do this! Stay at it! And remember what the Gunderson girls said to me: "Don't give up! Don't let her push you away. She needs you to stay close." They encouraged me to fight through the hard times, and to be assured that she really wants and needs her dad in her life, regardless of what she might say or do. With that in mind . . .

Engage, Maverick! After all, she is your prized possession!

Real Talk

"Every girl deserves to know she is a Prized Possession"

Acknowledgements

I would like to thank several people for their participation in this project. When I felt compelled to organize my thoughts on the father/daughter relationship, I really didn't know where this was going. I told several people, that "I don't know what the end game is for this." I just knew that I had to keep moving forward.

I call this a "project" rather than simply a book because I never set out to write a book. In the process of "moving forward," several components bubbled up. A book was only one of these components. The components of this project as of today are, 1. This book, 2. A website found at www.myfatherdaughter.com. 3. A weekly blog you can subscribe to from our website and 4. A live seminar for dads centered on the topic of fathers with daughters.

I am grateful to those who helped this project move forward.

Sharon Smyth, my awesome wife of 29 years has been an incredible support in my journey of learning how to be a dad. She was always very supportive of anything I ever wanted to do with Brittany growing up, including taking her to Hawaii. More than just being supportive of me in my role as Dad, she has been an incredible mother as well. While this book focusses on the important role a Dad has in the life of a daughter, the role of a great mom is huge as well. Sharon was and still is a fantastic mom which played a huge role in the success of our kids. She has been my #1 cheerleader of this project moving forward.

Brittany Smyth, my daughter, provided me with the laboratory I needed to work at being the dad she needed me to be. She has given me 25 great years and it has been my joy to be her dad. I am humbled by the chapter she wrote and blessed by her words.

Kristy Fox, my Young Life colleague and partner in this project, has played a huge role in all of this coming together. It was her seminar at camp that provided me with the platform I needed to begin this process. She has been encouraging and supportive of things moving forward and has contributed every step of the way. Her contribution of chapter 4 in this book as well as her collaboration in our live seminar along with her weekly blog entry makes her an integral part of this project.

Dr. Don Worcester, my friend and practicing counselor with his doctoral degree in Psychology, gave me important early encouragement during the formation of this project. When I still didn't know what this was, his professional experience and affirmation of the importance of this topic gave me the fuel I needed to continue the process. His weekly blog entries have been an important voice to our readers.

Rusty George, Lead Pastor of Real Life Church, provided some very important affirmation along the way. His words confirmed that this project was indeed worthwhile and needed. His encouragement of the book as well as our live seminar kept me going as I was looking for important early signs that this project was worthwhile. He kept me on track.

Donna Hatasaki, a longtime friend and gifted writer, provided a great sounding board and affirmation of the chapters that were being written. She has invested enormous amounts of time reading and responding during this process. Hers is a voice I valued greatly during the writing process and I appreciate her help, correction, support and encouragement.

Brad Voigt, of BradVoigt.com, was an important cog in the creation of this project. I ran into him "coincidentally" at Young Life camp just as things were coming together. He has built our website and provided lots of important coaching along the way along with some early encouragement and vision for what this could be.

Dozens of Dad's, Daughters & Leaders contributed their experiences and insights. There are too many to list here, but they know who they are. This project was never about just *my* thoughts. Bringing in dozens of others who all have an important perspective is the beauty of this project.

About the Authors

Sharon, Trevor, Brittany & Alan Smyth

Alan Smyth

I am a husband and a father who has had 25 years of experience raising a daughter. I didn't say "expertise," I said "experience." Beyond my own personal experience as a dad, I have been on the Young Life staff for 24 years giving me a front row seat to the lives of adolescent's (boys and girls). I have seen up close their issues and sometimes the sad consequences of their life choices. I am also in direct contact with hundreds of female Young Life staff and leaders who are intimately involved with girls as they struggle to grow up.

I have been married to me wife, Sharon, for 29 years and we have two awesome kids. Our daughter Brittany is 25 years old, a graduate from Point Loma Nazarene University in San Diego and is now out in the work force. She also enjoys serving on the South Central Los Angeles Young Life team where she helps to reach inner city, at risk youth in LA. Our son Trevor (20) is studying at the United States Naval Academy and playing football there. "Go NAVY, Beat ARMY!" I am a graduate of San Jose State University with a Communication Studies/Business degree. I have enjoyed my 24 years on the Young Life staff, a non-denominational Christian outreach, where I am currently serving as the Regional Director for the Greater Los Angeles Region. I love sports, my family, friends and giving my life to something a lot bigger than myself.

This book is the result of lots of God directed circumstances blended with my real life experiences of being a dad. I have a huge heart for being a dad to both of my kids. However, my heart breaks for girls who have been traumatize by our culture and have been dealt the raw deal of not having an engaged dad in their life. It would be my joy to somehow pass something useful along to younger dads who will in turn love their daughters in a more fulfilling, meaningful and Godly way.

I would love to hear from you as you navigate this important time in your life and as you interact with this content. Feel free to e-mail me from our website if you would like to enter into some dialogue concerning raising your daughter.

May God bless you in your efforts to be a great Dad! I pray this book can be helpful to you in the process.

Kristy Fox

Joshua, Jon, Luke, Kristy & Madeline Fox

I am a follower of Jesus, a wife, a mom, and have worked with teenagers (especially teenage girls) for the past 22 years. I have been married to my incredible husband and partner for 17 years and have 3 kids—Joshua, Madeline and Luke. I am a graduate of UC Irvine with a Social Science degree and minor in Political Science. I have had the privilege of walking with high school girls in deep relationships for the past 22 years—4 of those years as a volunteer within a church youth program and 18 years as a Young Life Area Director. I am currently serving in Young Life as the Regional Director for the South Coast Region which is San Diego and Orange County. I have enjoyed working with adolescent girls from all different socioeconomic, racial, religious and family backgrounds. I have remained working with young people directly for so long because my heart breaks and aches for young people and the exciting, yet difficult place they are in their life journey. I also love to read, travel, and spend time with my family!

Dr. Don Worcester

I am married to Renee and we have 4 great kids, Abigail (9), Emma (12), Jacob (14) and Keaton (21). I enjoy Spicy food, Bold Coffee, Fly Fishing, Frisbee Golf, Mesquite BBQ and the History Channel. I also enjoy speaking at Leadership Conferences, Parenting Seminars; and facilitating Marriage retreats with my wife Renee.

I have a Doctorate in Counseling Psychology from Northern Arizona University.

A Masters in Counseling from Arizona State University,

A Bachelors of Arts from Arizona State University.

I have spent the last 25 years working in Educational, Counseling and Organizational settings. I have taught in Public High schools and at the University level. I completed my Master's in Counseling degree in 1984 and have provided counseling services in Community based centers, in Adolescent Group homes, in Private practice and at Remuda Ranch Treatment Center; an intensive inpatient Residential program for adolescent girls and women seeking recovery from Eating disorders.

I was on staff with Young Life for 15 years where I worked as an Area Director; a Church Partner; a Regional Trainer, and developed and coordinated a National Staff Assessment program.

I currently provide services through my company, True North Consulting. The services include Speaking, Training, Coaching and Consulting. The focus is on helping people navigate their lives; Personally, Professionally and Spiritually.

Stay Connected

We would love to stay connected to you through your journey. Please visit our website often and communicate with us along the way. You will find a growing collection of resources there that are intended to encourage you in your journey as a dad. From our website, you can subscribe to our weekly blog where we regularly discuss various perspectives of the important and sacred task of raising a daughter.

Our Website: www.Myfatherdaughter.com

"Like" us on Facebook: Myfatherdaughter.com

Follow us on Twitter: Myfatherdaughter.com @2cor618

Purchase this book: You may purchase additional copies of this book from our website. Hard cover, paperback and digital formats are available.

Credits

Chapter 2—My Journey to Perspective, Insight & Conviction

1. Young Life, *A Non-denominational, International Christian Outreach Ministry,* www.younglife.org

Chapter 3—The Assault on our Girls

1. Mary Pipher, Ph.D., *Reviving Ophelia: Saving the Selves of Adolescent Girls* (New York: Riverhead Books, 1994), p. 12, 28
2. You Can Run . . . But You Cannot Hide! International, *Oh, Come On! It's Just Music!,* http://youcanruninternational.com/event_assemblies/under-the-influence.html.
3. Starr, Christine R, & Ferguson, Gail M. (2012). Sexy Dolls, Sexy Grade-schoolers? Media & Maternal Influences on Young Girls' Self-Sexualization. *Sex Roles: A Journal of Research,* 67(7-8), 463-476.
4. Tim McNulty, "Degrading lyrics lead to early sex, study says," *Pittsburgh Post-Gazette,* March 16, 2012, http://www.post-gazette.com/stories/sectionfront/life/degrading-lyrics-lead-to-early-sex-study-says-445168/#ixzz1xeGCeiBX.
5. The Dove Campaign For Real Beauty, "The Real Truth About Beauty: Revisited," www.dove.us/Social-Mission/campaign-for-real-beauty.aspx.

Chapter 4—Kristy's Seminar

1. Kate Fox, "Mirror, Mirror," *Social Issues Research Centre,*1997, www.sirc.org/publik/mirror.html

2. Melinda Brodbeck & Erin Evans, "Dove Campaign For Real Beauty Case Study," *Public Relations Problems & Cases,* March 5, 2007, http://psucomm473.blogspot.com/2007/03/dove-campaign-for-real-beauty-case.html.

Appendix

10 Rules for Dating my Daughter

1. Get a job
2. Understand I don't like you
3. I'm everywhere
4. You hurt her, I hurt you
5. Be home 30 minutes early
6. Get a lawyer
7. If you lie to me, I will find out
8. She's my princess, not your conquest
9. I don't mind going *back* to jail
10. Whatever you do to her, I will do to you

Application for Dating my Daughter

1. Name_____ DOB _____
2. Height _____ Weight ____ I.Q. _____ (If below 140, need not apply)
3. Athletic Accomplishments _____
4. Church you attend _____
5. In 50 words or less, explain what "DON'T TOUCH MY DAUGHTER" means.
6. In 50 words or less, explain what "LATE" means.
7. Complete the following:

   The last place I would want to be shot is _____

   If I were to be beaten, the last bone I would want broken is
   _____

   The one thing I hope this application doesn't ask is _____

8. What do you want to be IF you grow up?
9. Have you ever been fingerprinted?
10. Give location of any identifying birth marks or tattoos.
11. List all hard assets, liquid cash and financial liabilities.
12. (Over/Under) 25 times having seen Braveheart (If less than 5 times, need not apply)
13. Model & Make of the care you drive _____ (if a van, need not apply)

I hearby swear that all of the above information is true and correct to the best of my knowledge under penalty of death and / or dismemberment.

Signed _____

Thank you for your interest. Please allow 4-6 years for processing. You will be contacted in writing if you are approved. Please do not call, write or e-mail. Any contact during processing could cause a delay.

Letter From God to Your Daughter

Dearest Daughter,

You may not know me, but I know everything about you.[i] You were not a mistake, for all your days are written in my book.[ii] You are fearfully and wonderfully made.[iii] I knit you together in your mother's womb.[iv] And brought you forth on the day you were born.[v]

I am not distant and angry, but am the complete expression of love.[vi] And it is my desire to lavish my love on you.[vii] Simply because you are my child and I am your Father.[viii] I offer you more than your earthly father ever could.[ix] For I am the perfect father.[x]

You may think that I have forgotten you, but I have not . . . I cannot.[xi] My plan for your future has always been filled with hope. [xii] No purpose of mine can be thwarted . . . . And I have determined to do great and mighty works in you and through you . . . [xiii] Because I love you with an everlasting love.[xiv] My thoughts toward you are countless as the sand on the seashore.[xv] And I rejoice over you with singing.[xvi] I will never stop doing good to you.[xvii] And I want to show you great and marvelous things.[xviii] I am the Lord your God . . . and I am with you . . . I take great delight in you . . . I quiet you with my love . . . [xix] For I am your greatest encourager.[xx]

I am also the Father who comforts you in all your troubles.[xxi] When you are brokenhearted, I am especially near to you . . . . Closer than your own breath . . . [xxii] I weep with you and gather you in my arms like a little lamb . . . [xxiii] I am holding you close to my heart even now.

[xxiv] Pour out your heart to me, for I am your refuge . . . . You are safe in my everlasting arms.[xxv] One day I will wipe away every tear from your eyes. And I'll take away all the pain you have suffered on this earth.[xxvi]

Your job is to rest in my everlasting arms . . . . while I gaze upon you with tenderness and affection.[xxvii] Because I am your heavenly Father,[xxvii] And you are my deeply loved little child.[xxix] You are precious and honored in my sight . . . . I love you.[xxx]

Love,

Your Heavenly Father

[i] Psalm 139:1

[ii] Psalm 139:15-16

[iii] Psalm 139:14

[iv] Psalm 139:13

[v] Psalm 71:6

[vi] 1 John 4:16

[vii] 1 John 3:1

[viii] 1 John 3:1

[ix] Matthew 7:11

[x] Matthew 5:48

[xi] Isaiah 49:15

[xii] Jeremiah 29:11

[xiii] Job 42:2; Deuteronomy 3:24

[xiv] Jeremiah 31:3

[xv] Psalms 139:17-18

[xvi] Zephaniah 3:17

[xvii] Jeremiah 32:40

[xviii] Jeremiah 33:3

[xix] Zephaniah 3:17

[xx] 2 Thessalonians 2:16-17

[xxi] 2 Corinthians 1:3-4

[xxii] Psalm 34:18

[xxiii] Isaiah 40:11

[xxiv] Isaiah 40:11

[xxv] Psalm 62:8; Deuteronomy 33:27

[xxvi] Revelation 21:3-4

[xxvii] Isaiah 30:15; Isaiah 28:12; Deuteronomy 33:27)

[xxviii] 1 John 3:1; Romans 8:15

[xxix] 1 John 3:1; Romans 8:15

[xxx] Isaiah 43:4

The State of Our Girls

The following is a peek into the world of girls through those who have a front row seat. I am connected to hundreds of adult female staff and volunteers who, in turn, are in direct relationship with thousands of young girls and have been for many years. These staff and leaders have spent thousands of hours investing in the lives of junior high and high school girls. They have entered their lives and heard their stories. They have laughed and cried with their younger friends. I asked a number of these leaders to share with me some thoughts, quotes, and impressions regarding the state of our girls' relationships with their dads—or lack thereof. The following is a compilation of their responses. The words below come directly from dozens of women as they relay what they have personally seen. A special thank you to those heroes who pursue hurting young women every day, and were kind enough to share their thoughts that are found below. For obvious reasons, I have omitted all names.

As society and culture takes its toll on girls today, girls begin to lose a sense of their own value. It's a painful loss and often leads to a search for painkillers. Alcohol and drugs are often used to numb the pain. Girls compromise their God-given value to meet the expectations of boys who can't possibly understand the beautiful treasures God has created them to be. "If I only give my boyfriend what he wants," they think, "then I'll matter. I'll be something, I'll belong." The problem is, such a pattern reduces a girl to her ability to perform and her willingness to have sex. Such a degradation of her identity will act as a huge wall against her understanding of who God has created her to be and the value He, as her Father, has placed on her life.

We are seeing physically or verbally abusive fathers. Among other things, they communicate, "You are worthless. I wish that you didn't exist." In response, these daughters often feel inadequate. They long to fix their father's problems, and when they are unable to change the behavior, they feel like failures. These girls grow up with an unhealthy fear of men and a spirit of submission that neglects their rightful place in a relationship. They often fall into relationships where men use them and abuse them, objectifying them and treating them as if they live to serve.

We are seeing sexually abusive fathers. This communicates, "You are nothing but the object of my sexual craving. Your inner beauty, your talents, your dreams do not matter to me. You are my secret and I hold you in my power for as long you keep quiet. I do not care about your future or your brokenness. You are my slave." In response, these daughters suffer from a deep emotional brokenness that is often compounded by the chains of secrecy. They are alone and often disengage from peers and feel they cannot open up to adults for fear of betraying their father. "I didn't think he really wanted to hurt me so I didn't tell anyone. I was scared and alone, but I convinced myself that this was normal. This was how every father treated his daughter." Suffering alone, these girls carry heavy burdens that often come out after years of suppression and denial. The terror and ache from such abuse at the hand of an important male figure can even cause girls to form a fear of men. "I had just been hurt by too many guys in my life, I knew I could never learn to love one, but I longed to love and be loved."

We are seeing neglectful fathers. They communicate, "I am sorry that I ever conceived you. You are a mistake. I have no time or energy to comfort, protect or love you. You are a bother and a burden. If only there was something more to you that could keep my attention, something worth loving." In response, these daughters spend a majority of their focus on proving their worth. They pour themselves into being the best at any sport, or talent, or academic endeavor in order to be held valuable in the eyes of their father. They obsess over being perfect, fearing that mistakes will drive away the attention that they crave. They are constantly forced to face what they lack and what they should have/could have been or done. They are constantly reminded of what they are not, instead of all the many amazing things they are. They grow with a fear of abandonment and a lack of trust in people. It is better not to trust anyone and protect themselves from being hurt again, than to invest in someone and be left raw and wounded when they leave. The fear of abandonment cripples many women who have not only been neglected by a father figure, but have watched their mothers suffer in the absence of a husband as well.

From a high school age girl: "Because of my experience, my perception of God altered my reality and made me act stubbornly. I didn't trust who He was. I didn't trust how He saw me. I didn't feel valuable or precious in His eyes. I felt like I was expendable."

At the age of ten, "V" lost her mom to cancer. When Mom found out she was sick, V's dad left mom and moved in with another woman. Two weeks after Mom died, Dad married that woman, and began the second of five marriages she saw her dad go through during her high school life. V's dad was physically in their home, but might as well have not been. V does not trust men. She believes they are all generally bad. Her father modeled to her that if you aren't good or perfect as a woman, then the man will flee to pursue something better. V is now 26, and still refuses to allow men to be anything more than friends. She doesn't believe there is a healthy relationship beyond that. V had to be the parent to her two younger sisters, both of whom have been very sexually active since a young age.

When "K" was young, her dad left home, and she saw him every other weekend. K loved her dad, but never felt good enough. She blamed herself for his leaving. During K's junior year of high school, she told me that she had been drinking heavily. This surprised me, because she wasn't in the party crowd at all. She drank alone. She drank in her room before and after school. She needed "the confidence alcohol gave" to get through an ordinary day. She only drank hard alcohol that she had hidden in places throughout her house. K has a hard time accepting love, because she doesn't feel worthy of it. I believe the hard relationship with her dad made her feel that she had to perform to be able to be loved.

"B" has been without her dad since she was three. She sees him once a year for a week, and has no other contact with him besides the forced court visit. She hates visiting her dad. She is second-best to his new wife while she is there, and she gets very little attention or time with her dad. B is one of the most guarded girls I have ever been in contact with. I have spent three years meeting with her and investing in her. She has enormous walls up with everyone. B has a lot of people in her life—all surface level relationships. She can't allow anyone to get close to her because they all leave her. She is one of the most beautiful girls I have ever met—she's stunning, honestly. She intentionally dresses very provocatively to get the attention of the opposite sex. She literally flaunts herself and loves the attention men give her because of this. I have seen her attract many guys over the course of the years, and she gives herself physically to all of them. This is what she thinks love is, because "men use women." She struggles with her feelings a lot, and when she doesn't like what she feels or if it hurts too much, she cuts herself so she can control her pain. This mostly happens before she has to go see her dad. She counts the days until she is 18 and can decide that she doesn't have to spend time with "someone who has never loved or cared about me." B is what I would call a party girl, using most anything she can to numb herself.

My dad is lazy and absent from my life. Although he is home, he sits around watching TV or doing other things rather than spend time with our family. He only communicates with me when he is mad at me for something I have done. When he knows he has done something that upsets my brother or me, he tries to buy our love back by getting us presents. He gave me a gift a few months ago that is still sitting in my closet. It's still wrapped, because I don't even care enough to open it. I can't even look at it because it makes me so angry. I don't understand why he treats my mom the way he does when she works so hard for our family and is such an amazing woman.

My dad was my best friend growing up. When my mom and I fought, he would sneak me out and get me ice cream or take me to lunch so I could get away from her. My dad passed away last year, and I haven't felt like the same person since. I feel numb and hardly have any emotion to anything that goes on around me. I've lost the spunk and joy I once had, and I don't know how to get it back.

My dad is in jail. He has been since I was young. It's hard to know that I will never be able to see him without a piece of glass between us. I won't be able to hug him for a long time, or have him at my wedding.

I don't even know who my dad is.

One teenager I know who was raised away from her dad, and whose mother slept around with multiple men, has come to the brink of danger. For starters, she isn't very smart, but when synthesized with a strong desire to be loved where no love was given, she turned to having sex with as many guys who were willing. She was repeatedly caught having sex with multiple guys at the same time, on school grounds. She was eventually expelled. The mother also came from a home lacking a father figure. The only two males in her life growing up were her a younger brother and drunk grandpa.

I talked to a 17-year-old girl yesterday who was raised in a very loving family. The problem is, the parents love her more than each other. This creates anxiety in her home, because she is about to graduate next year and she is concerned that they will divorce when she leaves. I see many empty-nesters splitting up because their marriage was centered on the child and not the marriage. I think this domestic anxiety can turn the child inward or away from the family unit. In the case of this teen, it is the latter. She doesn't see the value of marriage and doesn't believe in love—just a partnership.

Another girl I have talked to comes from a terribly broken home. Her mom has been through two husbands and each ended in heartbreak. Now, the girl doesn't believe in marriage but just living with a guy. She saw the pain in marriage and wants to avoid that pain by not marrying.

In my 16 years of leading Young Life, I can tie nearly every single girl's self-confidence to her relationship with her dad. Everyone wants approval, but the approval of a father for his daughter is beyond impactful. I have had girls verbalize that they are having sex with their boyfriends to get their dads' attention, to prove to their dad that they are worthy of being loved, to show their dad someone wants them, or to make their dad feel like what he thinks of her doesn't matter.

I have seen them turn to any male attention they can get, and flirt inappropriately with older men. I had one girl who got wrapped up in an affair with a teacher because she was so desperate to have some male find her worthy. Another made advances on a friend's dad, because he was kind to her and she thought that was appropriate. (Her own dad had an affair with a younger woman.) One girl threatened to take her own life because her dad left her family for another family. I've seen girls so desperate to have a relationship with their dads that they destroy their relationship with their moms because they blame the mom for Dad's lack of attention and interest.

Most of the promiscuity I've seen in my girls can be attributed to a lack of a father figure pouring into her. I have a girl who has a great, godly dad who loves her, but he's so wrapped up in his boys and their sports and his work that she doesn't feel invested in. She resents him. She has turned to a way of life she doesn't even want. I have several girls who don't believe in long-term relationships because their parents aren't together anymore. They think leaving someone is how life is meant to be. Even those girls who have dads that are good to them are greatly affected by how the dad treats the mom.

In another vein, when a girl begins to hear and learn who God is, she almost always associates her father with a picture of who God is. I spend a lot of time talking through the fact that as humans we fail, but our heavenly Father never fails. If a girl hasn't experienced tangible love and investment from her dad (touch, affirmation, value, unconditional support, discipline), then it's really hard for her to trust in the love of God.

One of the most heartbreaking stories I've heard was from a girl whose dad left when she was a baby. She has been raised by her step-dad, and she calls him "Dad." She has longed for his acceptance her entire life. However, recently he told her in so many words that he didn't need to worry about how she "turned out," because she wasn't really his daughter. Heartbreaking news to her. She believed she was. She needed to be claimed, unconditionally loved, and seen as "his."

Several years ago, I showed up at a high school student's house to pick her up. As I walked up to the door, her little sister was out front on the porch with a backpack. I asked her what she was doing, and she said she was waiting for her dad to pick her up. She continued to tell me that he was coming to get her for the weekend, and how excited she was. I walked inside and her older sister said, "My dad won't come." I looked at her with questioning eyes, and she said that her sister waits there a couple times a month, and dad never shows up. Never. He makes plans with her and never shows up. My high school friend told me that she, too, used to wait and wait, but then she gave up. She now has no expectations, no hopes and no trust.

I watched a movie the other day, in which a teenage boy said, "It's the worst" when dads try too hard. A teenage girl looked at him and said, "No, what would be worse is if they didn't try at all."

One girl who comes to mind was from a broken family but lived with her dad. Her mom had psych issues and was out of the picture. Dad was heartbroken, detached, and unavailable. She turned her attention to boys. She had a very unhealthy relationship with a boyfriend, having sex and experimenting with drugs. When asked about the relationship she would say things like, "My dad doesn't know or care what I do. He never asks me about my life or how I am doing. At least my boyfriend loves me and helps me through things." She was crying out for love from her father. I'd like to hope he had the best intentions, but he seemed to be too intimidated by all the issues that go along with raising a teen girl. He didn't know his part or boundaries. Instead of stepping in in any way, he kept a distance and therefore missed out on healing, loving, and sharing the heart of his beautiful daughter. Both parties left empty. So heartbreaking.

This is a hard topic to focus my thoughts on, because it hits so close to home for me. I have such a wonderful relationship with my own father, and I can clearly see the impact that relationship had on my own life. Coming from that experience makes it hard to see the obstacles some of my girls face in their lives due to absent fathers (both absent by choice and absent by death). Some of the things I have heard girls say are:

"I know my dad is looking down on me and is upset with how I behave with boys."

"If my dad were around, my life would be easier."

"If my Dad were around, I wouldn't get away with the things I get away with."

I have seen the ramifications of no father figure show up in many ways: confidence/self-esteem, relationship issues, sexuality, school performance, future plans—all with negative results. At times, girls will even acknowledge that they are making a poor decision, and place blame on their absent fathers.

It seems to me that the most consistent theme of poor choices that directly correlate to absent fathers is in their relationships with men. I think that is a pretty consistent observation, and not uncommon when you think of the two together.

Here are a few things my kids from various ministry setting have said:

"I am afraid of getting married, because if I wasn't enough to keep my dad around, then how could I be enough to keep a husband around?"

"I don't know if I will be able to trust a man, since I've never been able to trust my dad."

"I don't think I will be good in a marriage, because I'm so used to taking care of myself since my dad left. I don't think I would have any use for a husband."

"I won't ever need a man. I never needed my dad."

"I don't want to open up to a man because I'm afraid he will just hurt me like my dad."

Below are some of my observations and the consequences of fathers who were physically and/or emotionally absent. When Dad is not present physically and/or emotionally (both are so important!), young girls are so sad and empty. When these girls become teens, this lack of approval, acceptance, protection, and love, creates a huge hunger and deep need for approval, acceptance, protection, and love from other men. Often, but not always, this displays itself in searching for love in all the wrong places . . . unhealthy relationships with young men (even willing to put up with abusive relationships), promiscuity, excessive partying, etc. Of course, all of these lead to very troubling outcomes/consequences, including abusive relationships, teen pregnancy, substance abuse/addictions, poor school performance, etc. I have also seen some of these issues with teens with special needs who have a lack of a father figure. In fact, 80% of marriages with a child with a special need end in divorce, so many of these teens (and their siblings) manage life with a single parent.

I remember driving one of my girls home many years ago. She was a gorgeous gal, very popular with the guys, and everyone envied her because she was allowed to stay out as long as she wanted on any given night. When I drove her home that night, she broke down in tears, expressing the envy of others. She said that what they didn't know or understand was that the reason she could do whatever she wanted, was because no parent was ever home to see if she got in okay at night. Her parents were divorced, and her mother often spent the night at a boyfriend's home. This sweet yet troubled girl said through her tears that she just wished someone was home at night to care. She would have given everything she had for a curfew. She felt so alone, and just wanted someone at home who cared enough to be there for her.

All of this seems well-documented and expected, given the situation. I do, however, think there is a smaller percentage of girls who, in their heartache of an absentee father, pull in a different direction. This is a quieter segment of the population but no less important. In their search for approval, acceptance, love, and control, they handle their emptiness by being over-achievers (in school, sports, extra-curricular activities, etc.), by being overly concerned about appearance (leading to bulimia and anorexia), and by focusing on success as their approval/fulfillment. I've noticed that as these girls mature and age, their consequences and outcomes are more subtle, yet no less severe. Being over-achievers with high expectations often leads these girls to difficulty in finding a husband who meets their standards, and/or finding it difficult to stay married. Their focus on superficiality (appearance, etc.) can lead to bulimia, anorexia, various plastic surgeries, exercise addiction, and more. This image of outward super-success with an empty interior can eventually lead to a crash later in life, such as divorce, breakdown, affairs, depression, self-inflicted injuries, substance abuse, etc.

Fathers are almost nonexistent for the children in South Central Los Angeles. A girl whose father is present is extremely rare. Of the girls who don't have a present father, most have no idea who he is. Girls who do know their fathers usually only know him to be in and out of their lives, if he is around at all. In South Central, there is hardly any divorce, but that's because there is hardly any marriage.

Another harsh reality: a lot of these girls have been sexually abused. When there are absent fathers, many of the girls' mothers have male relatives that live with them, bring new boyfriends into the house, or simply leave their kids with the wrong person. I've watched this greatly affect the girls' self-worth and how it has led to most of them becoming sexually active at a young age or turning to drinking and smoking as a way to cope and forget what was done to them.

One young gal has been shuttled back and forth between parents since the first grade. Their nasty divorce, coupled her emotional issues (she inherited the anger characteristics of the father), has led her to years in counseling. She continues to live with that sense of abandonment. It's not that her father, who now lives in Wisconsin while she's in California, doesn't visit. But when she is with him, he is completely emotionally and socially unavailable to her. She just wants him to hug her, and tell her that she's beautiful, advise her in life, and be an encouraging Dad to her. Instead, she gets criticism, and made to feel that she's a problem in his life.

Regardless of her emotional instability, he cannot give her anything that she needs in a dad. Next week, she's going for a weeklong visit with him, and she's starting to act out from the anxiety that she is facing and the fear she will continue to be reminded what she doesn't get from him. Here is an example of a dad who pays some bills and sees that as being a father. She's starving, and Christ is her only hope to know how life can be different for her and her future.

Another young lady would love to have her dad be more than a coach. For him, it's all about the win. Mom and Dad are together in a pretty great family, but he won't talk to her about anything other than how she can be a better soccer player or get straight A's. She is flirtatious with all boys, just dying to hear something wonderful about herself. Again, he is a present father, but not one who is equipping her to become a woman. She mentioned to me that at camp it became obvious to her that she wasn't being raised right. She said she wishes that her parents didn't give her everything she wants, and would spend more time teaching her how to do life.

I know another young girl who only knows anger from her father, and lives in fear of him. A restraining order keeps him away from that home, and she lives in fear of him and his antics. She knows him to lie and go to great lengths to manipulate. While she waits for the pending divorce that has been ongoing for three years now, she has no healthy male role models. I see her taking on masculine characteristics, and acting like a husband for her mother in how she nurtures and comforts her in this mess. She has no instruction at all in how to grow to be a woman of honor and great character.

Lack of self worth. Girls often feel their fathers reject being a part of their lives because of something they did. There is no explanation you can give them that changes this false thinking. If their parent rejects them, they blame themselves. These girls lack self-confidence and don't feel they are smart, talented, or loveable. They are often withdrawn, and they need people in their lives to encourage them and make them realize that they have many gifts and talents. Many times, they don't trust any relationships or have close friendships, because they are afraid of loss. I always tell girls that their dads are the ones missing out on how great they are, but I don't know if they can really receive those words.

Lack of confidence. I feel that strong, confident girls have a great foundation from their relationships with their fathers. A girl needs to know that her father believes in her, thinks she is beautiful, and loves her unconditionally. If this isn't happening on an ongoing basis in a girl's life, she lacks confidence and won't put herself out there when it comes to trying new things, or being involved in extracurricular activities. Girls don't think they can accomplish things when they don't think anyone believes in them. There is something unique and vital about a father expressing his approval and support to his daughter. I had a student whose father was present in her life, but always put her down. He told her that she dressed like a slut, and that she wasn't going to go far in life. She became overly obsessed with her body image, struggled with eating disorders, did not finish high school, and has had many bad relationships with males. She gave up on herself, and felt that her parents had given up on her early on.

Seeking attention from males. Girls without father figures often seek attention from men, and will be overly eager to have a boyfriend or girlfriend. They search for some sort of connection to someone else. They are often more willing to have sexual relationships, and even desire getting pregnant to have someone that will love them. I had a 15-year-old student whose dad is in jail, and is abusive to her when he has been out of jail. She is in a very unhealthy relationship with an older boy and is very dependent on him. She ended up getting pregnant, and now lives with him and his mother. She needed that "permanent" connection to someone, and, as unhealthy as it is with her boyfriend, it's someone to belong to.

Difficulty believing that God loves them. A father is the first example to his children of God's love. If there is not a loving relationship between a girl and her father, the girl will have a hard time understanding that her Father, God, loves her unconditionally. I had so many Young Life girls who had no father in their lives and had such a hard time really trusting that God loved them unconditionally. They really had a hard time understanding forgiveness, and felt that God would reject them if they made mistakes.

Confusing roles in their families. Often when a girl has younger siblings in the home and no father, the mother in the home will rely on the older sibling to help her raise her sisters and brothers. I have seen parents pull their kids out of traditional high school and enroll them in a continuation school, just to be able to be home and take care of her younger siblings. This puts a tremendous strain on the teenage girl, as she feels responsible for her siblings and therefore does not have a lot of time for her own activities and desires. Often, the mother will have other relationships with men coming and going from the teenage girls' lives. I saw this a lot with my students. The mothers were often preoccupied with these new relationships, so the girls would get frustrated when a new person was in the house trying to parent them. This causes a lot of tension and feelings of rejection from their mothers as well as their fathers. Stepfathers can really be a blessing to these girls, if they can understand their new role and build encouraging relationships with the girls and not expect to replace their father or be an authoritarian right away. I have had students who really flourish with their stepfathers, but in most cases, the girls do not accept them. They feel they don't have strong relationships with their stepfathers. It's just a hard dynamic when a new man becomes a stepfather to a teenage girl.

I truly believe that the relationship between a father and his daughter is the most important relationship she will have in her life. It is the foundation of how she will view herself and all of her relationships in the future, including her relationship with God. If there is rejection by her father, I believe it is a lifelong struggle for the girl to believe in herself and feel lovable.

The girls I am in relationship with are struggling in many ways. Many of them are really needy and are looking for anyone to get hugs from. They are looking for people to tell them everything that is going on in their lives. They try to get close to our guy leaders, and reveal personal information to them. Many have never had a father figure in their lives. Their families are known for having many moves within neighborhoods, which indicated a lot of instability.

Many of our girls are always talking about boyfriends and have their self-esteem at an all time low because they feel like no one has ever cared about them. We have found that many of our girls cut themselves. I have seen the scars on their wrists. Sometimes, they are very emotionally attached to their scars, and don't necessarily see them as a bad thing. They would get the blades from their moms' drawers, and their moms knew it.

I texted "K" to see how she was. She told me that she had broken her leg, and when I asked her what happened, she said that she'd jumped off her roof. "Why did you jump off the roof?" I asked, and she told me that she was trying to kill herself. I reassured her of God's love for her, and said that no matter how alone she felt, she would never be alone. She's still obsessed with having boyfriends, and she makes them first in her world because of her longing for a male figure in her life.

Another story is that of "C". She told me that her mom hated her, and that her mom blamed her for the breakup of their marriage. "C" felt unwanted in her home. She was an outcast at home and school. Once, when I asked her how she was doing, she told me that she had just gotten out of the hospital, because she'd tried to kill herself by taking a bottle of pills. She was crying for attention. She wanted to numb the pain of the void she had in her heart for a real mom and dad. She wanted so badly just to be loved by her parents. She had grown up in this tough environment.

I have had the blessing to work with a diverse set of girls. Growing up in Los Angeles, absent fathers are the norm. The result is that girls seek acceptance from males, often in unhealthy forms. They don't have a standard for what a good guy is. The lack of a father figure is not just for the young girls, but for the young boys as well. In Lennox, there are six strip clubs and eight adult video stores. Having these places near the libraries, schools, and even the sheriff station implies that the objectification of women is acceptable behavior. When there isn't a father figure to tell them otherwise, boys start going down the wrong path, which also affects our girls. Marriage is lost on them and premarital sex is condoned. When teen pregnancy happens, it is rare that the father of the baby will take responsibility and stick around.

From Alan: To sum things up, these are just a few snapshots of real life stories being told by those intimately involved. Sadly, we could go on all day. I also asked a number of friends to survey the teenage girls that they work with. I asked three questions, and I've compiled many of their answers below.

1. What do you need most from your dad?

Support.
I need my dad's guidance and advice and never ending love. I need to think that I'm a princess.
I need guidance and most of all love. Trust is good too.
More attention.
Support with things I'm struggling with.
For him to be home more often and care for me.
Understanding.

For him to be there and love me.

Respect, love and trust.

To love me, to not compare me to others.

To not just buy me things, but to spend time with me.

To be worthy of the hero that he is in my head.

To be at my games.

To remember to ask me about the things I share with him.

To be okay with the fact that I'm a girl.

Choose me before work.

Attention.

For him to be a consistent loving factor in my life.

Show that he loves us even though I know he does.

Guidance.

2. What do you wish your dad knew about you?

More about my personal life, like with friends and boys. Also my relationship with God.

That I love him no matter how much we play fight or how much he pushes me.

I wish he knew that I'm not as confident as I seem, and that I am sometimes faced with a lot of pressures.

That I'm not as tough as he might think.

How he was when he was younger.

How much I love him.

Tough times I'm going through.

That I like when he's there for me.

I don't like when he drinks.

What I do on the weekends and understand why.

Less anger would help.

His opinion is really important to me.

He has the ability to make or break my day.

My confidence comes from how he treats me.

I need him to be my dad not my friend.

It matters a lot what others think of me.

I'm not sure I'm worth it (in general).

3. What do you wish your dad did differently?

I wish he was more understanding and didn't work as much, especially when I was younger.

I wish he wouldn't pick so many fights.

I wish he visited more.

Talk to me more.

Acting like he knows everything, expecting me to be perfect.

I wish he would come home.

Listen more.

Didn't yell at my mom or siblings.

More open-minded, understood me better.

Didn't brush me off because I'm not a son.

Put down his phone when he talked to me.

Treated my mom nicer.

Spent one on one time with me.

These words come directly from teenage girls who were speaking candidly about their dads. This chapter emphasizes the premise I am hoping to convey: that a positive, healthy, involved dad is absolutely critical to the healthy development of our girls. Being a male myself, I don't fully understand it, but I believe the dozens of stories that were told in this chapter.

Let me answer the question, "What is the state of our girls?" For girls who have an engaged, loving, supportive dad in their lives, the condition is good, if not great. They are generally happy, healthy, and productive. But for those tragically many girls who are not fortunate in this way, life is often hollow, lost, and a wreck. They are deeply wounded, and they will spend the rest of their lives healing. Society is pressing in on our girls, and when Dad is not present to defend, protect, and encourage, a gaping hole is left within the soul of a girl.

CPSIA information can be obtained at www.ICGtesting.com
Printed in the USA
BVOW070135220513

321326BV00002B/10/P